W9-BNT-861

ON METHOD ACTING

An actor's instrument is his whole self. It is his body, his mind and being, complete with thoughts, emotions, sensitivity, imagination, honesty, and awareness. Try to imagine the actor's instrument in much the same way you picture the musician and his violin, the artist and his canvas, paints, and brushes. Think of them as one and inseparable. Just as the musician practices daily on his instrument, always perfecting its response to his will through training, and the artist mixes his paints, brushing them on with the precision and beauty accrued only by drill, so must the actor be concerned with the training and development of his instrument and its responses to his commands.

ON
METHOD
ACTING

by EDWARD DWIGHT EASTY

IVY BOOKS • NEW YORK

Sale of this book without a front cover may be unauthorized. If this book is coverless, it may have been reported to the publisher as "unsold or destroyed" and neither the author nor the publisher may have received payment for it.

An Ivy Book
Published by The Random House Publishing Group
Copyright © 1981 by The House of Collectibles, Inc.

All rights reserved.

Published in the United States by Ivy Books, an imprint of The Random House Publishing Group, a division of Random House, Inc., New York, and simultaneously in Canada by Random House of Canada Limited, Toronto.

No part of this book may be reproduced or utilized in any form or by any means, electronic or mechanical, including photocopying, recording, or by any information storage and retrieval system, without permission in writing from the publisher.

Ivy Books and colophon are trademarks of Random House, Inc.

www.ballantinebooks.com

Library of Congress Catalog Card Number: 78-61740

ISBN 0-8041-0522-7

Manufactured in the United States of America

First Ballantine Books Edition: September 1989
Fourth Printing: January 1992

OPM 30 29 28 27 26 25 24 23

Foreword

In the mid-'thirties, as a freshman at Northwestern University at a time when the American theatre was largely a commercial flight away from reality, I saw a play out of the Goodman Theatre in Chicago that changed a lot of lives, including my own.

It began when I walked into the theatre and felt a tenseness, an animal excitement in the air that I associated more with a sports arena before a championship fight than with the rustle of playbills and small talk that preceded the few commercial plays I had seen.

There was no curtain. The actors, or *were* they actors, were seated in a semi-circle on a bare stage. Others had been liberally planted in the audience. A tough looking character who looked like one of Al Capone's "torpedoes" from the nearby south side, lolled against the proscenium, arrogantly picking his teeth and sizing up the audience.

Then with no dimming of lights, it began to happen. A man, slob fat, was standing downstage center, his hands raised for quiet. *Then* it began to happen. He was blasted from the audience with defiance, with catcalls, whistles, boos. And I can hear that fog horn of a voice still bellowing over the defiance into the four corners of what was now not a theatre but a Union Hall, and we were members, we were *there*: "You're so wrong, I ain't laughing!"

What followed in that small packed space was not so much a play as an experience, a galvanizing, unforgettable experience that had us all on our feet at the end wholly involved in one of the life and death social realities of the 'thirties, shouting: "STRIKE! STRIKE! STRIKE!"

The play was WAITING FOR LEFTY by Clifford Odets, a member of the Group Theatre which was a community of working artists under the leadership of Harold Clurman, Cheryl Crawford and Lee Strasberg. These three exceptional people were committed to a serious theatre rooted in an awareness of the individual and social realities of the time, and to a systematic training of actors to use themselves creatively as instruments in working for truth and reality on the stage. Alive and growing experimentally for some time, the Group Theatre was now ready in the year 1935 to take a dramatic giant step forward.

With WAITING FOR LEFTY, AWAKE AND SING, TILL THE DAY I DIE, and PARADISE LOST, all by Odets and all produced in a single year, the Group captured the direction of the American theatre, stood four square against its commercial flight away from reality, and opened up a new world of creative possibilities for writers, directors and actors.

And although the Group was dissolved in 1941, its experiment and its achievement remains a dominant one in the American theatre. In one area, certainly, it has permanently altered the course of its history. This area is defined in this book by Mr. Easty.

Out of the Group emerged one of theatre's finest artists, undoubtedly the greatest American teacher of acting in our time, Mr. Lee Strasberg. His work and influence in the modification, development and practical application of Stanislavsky's System of training actors to use themselves consciously as instruments to attain truth and reality on stage is now general and decisive. In fact, it might be hard to find an American actor of stature who has not been influenced directly or indirectly by Mr. Strasberg's years in the theatre. For twenty years, Mr. Strasberg has conducted classes in acting. In that time, by the hundreds each year, students and working actors have enrolled to learn and to work; to absorb what they can of Method acting from its greatest teacher. One such student was Edward Easty, the writer of this book. He studied with Strasberg for over a decade. Out of that experience, he has written this book on Method acting. Written for the layman as well as for the young actor, it has two great virtues in a difficult and often murky field—it covers the ground with simplicity and with clarity. And it *does* cover the ground.

It is more than a reference book on the Method, although it can be used most profitably as such; it is much more than a book by a student who has learned his lessons well. It is *Mr. Easty's* instrument, as it were, working well and creatively when he wrote this book. He had assimilated his years with Mr. Strasberg, years packed with creative experience, and out of it, with perception, organization, and a special talent for the task, he has written a book eminently readable as prose. It moves along in an exciting and provocative way. It is beautifully detailed. His ability to follow an actor's thought process while engaged in a specific task, the questions that must be answered if he is to attain reality in his work, should be of tremendous value to the actor who is just entering the mazes of the Method. In short, the book has a sound and style of its own.

I have not exhausted the virtues of Mr. Easty's ON METHOD ACTING. His relating the truth and reality of an actor's art to the truth and reality with which he lives his daily life, the book's keen and dramatic sense of anecdote, and the sections on Marilyn Monroe and James Dean are all beautifully conceived.

I will say that it ought to be required reading for young actors or the layman who wishes to understand the "mysteries" of Method acting in clear and simple terms. And that is as far as I go. The book that follows speaks most eloquently for itself.

ROBERT HERRIDGE

Contents

Introduction

Upon reaching the end of my writing of this book, I realized that there is much more that could possibly have been said on the subject. I want to say more but at the same time know that one book, or even volumes, cannot say it all; for art grows faster than all the writers of the world can record it. The salient facets of Konstantin Sergeyevich Stanislavsky's System as it has evolved to us today are the only parts I have discussed in this book. They are the very basis of the modern Method teacher's way of teaching. Those readers familiar with Stanislavsky's writings will ask what has happened to other aspects of his teachings. I can only answer that the facets set forth in this book are the ones in general use today by the leading proponents of his system. The rest of his teachings are either incorporated into what I have included or have been dropped because of their impracticality for the Western theatre.

The main facets of the Method as I have outlined them are in fact more than just facets of anything. They are basic principles which should be applied to the personality of the individual actor as well as to his role. I say this because they are sound and healthy principles; ones that if transgressed will stay any creative and artistic progress in the future development of the actor. Also, if any of them are violated, it will mean that the others will soon fall by the wayside. Their interdependency is fairly obvious.

I have broken the Method down into its familiar groupings

1

and tried to present them in a manner easily understood by the layman as well as the serious student of acting.

As for the use of this book, I would say that it is more desirable for an actor who is studying with a Method teacher to use this book either for an easier understanding of his studies or as a reference. This is particularly true for the exercises as outlined, but it can also be used by the person interested in learning what the Method is all about. So much has been said and written about it, usually by people who are prone to criticize something they regard as mystical, something they do not understand and have not taken the time to learn.

All books by Stanislavsky should be read by the serious acting student. An intellectual understanding of his system is necessary, but also an understanding of why there have been changes in it is equally important. However, an intellectual understanding is hardly enough. It must be applied, but this cannot be done without first learning how to apply it. This can only be done with the aid of a teacher who adheres to *all* facets of Stanislavsky's system as they have evolved; a teacher who conducts regular classes that will train and develop the actor's instrument. It definitely cannot be studied alone, unfortunately, and for this reason classes are necessary.

Just as this book is not meant to be a definitive analysis of the Method, neither is the Method meant to be a definitive end to learning how to act. Some say the Method has more benefits for the professional and experienced actor than for the beginner (the one who *knows* he can act because he has been doing it for so many years). Others say that the student who begins his studies with a Method teacher, without having first learned other techniques of acting from schools with an opposite point of view from ours, will benefit more because he does not have to tear down all the falsities in acting which he has previously learned. I say it clearly depends upon the individual, his trust in the Method, his teacher and his desire to learn.

Throughout this book I have perhaps let my personal feelings interject themselves with regard to proponents of other systems and techniques of acting. I freely admit that this is subjectivity on my part, but I have also tried to point up the faults of some Method actors and some faults easily slipped into *by* Method actors. God knows, there is nothing more reviling to watch than an actor who is *obviously* a Method actor!

A case in point concerns an actor, who, incidentally, has always been a favorite of mine and I still regard him as one of the great talents of the day. However, he too let himself be carried away in his "realistic" interpretation of a role. This sometimes happens to us. I am sure that it was his fervor for realism that led him astray from the author's lines.

A few years ago this particular actor was doing the title role in a New York production of Shakespeare's *King Lear*. His performance was breathtakingly perceptive to a point, but it was here that he veered from the tasks he had set for himself with what appeared to be done only as a vain attempt at originality. It was enough to destroy any reality previously formulated by those watching. It happened in the scene after the death of Cordelia. Lear, on seeing her body, cries in a grief stricken voice, "Why should a dog, a horse, a rat have life and thou no breath at all?—Thou'lt come no more." Then he utters his towering, fivefold, "never, never, never, never, never!"

However, when our friend got to the fifth "never" he spelled it out, "n-e-v-e-r."

Now this only serves to show how some Method actors let themselves be carried away by a sincere desire to be original. Clearly this reading of such a powerful and rather difficult speech was not intended to be done this way by Shakespeare or he would have said so. Even though it could have been read this way by any actor, it was read that way by a Method actor who was definitely influenced in a rather distorted manner by his way of teaching. Any perceptive person will realize that this could happen to anybody, but at the same time points up the need to keep a clear picture of the purpose of the Method. It was never designed to be the answer to all acting problems as most of these lie with the outside forces that steer the course of events in the theatre world.

It can help those problems which lie within the actor's personality but only if he honestly wants to be helped. Again, the Method is not the final result in acting, only the path to be taken to reach the pinnacle in his art.

Why a Method

A renaissance in acting has begun in America. This rebirth of artistic interest that clamors for truthfulness and reality in the art of acting began on a grand scale with Lee Strasberg's unbroken advancements in Konstantin S. Stanislavsky's System.

Lee Strasberg's early guidance with the old Group Theatre in the Thirties was only the beginning of a way of teaching acting in this country that would spread from coast to coast until we now hear the System, or Method, as it is better known, discussed by laymen as well as people in the theatre. Through Strasberg's leadership, the Method has emerged from its early insularity and has taken the front in modern theatre. Its influence has been felt not only by thousands of young people starting on a theatre career, but by actors of stellar category.

Many ''stars'' have taken indefinite leaves of absence from immediate work, some as long as two years, in order to study and begin their craft anew with a freshness and sense of truth that they knew was missing from their work. The present day Actors' Studio, and its recently purchased Hudson Theatre, was begun strictly as a place where the Method could be learned, applied, and then presented to the people.

The impact of the Method is by no means limited to actors alone. The world's finest legitimate stage directors, as well as some of the best movie directors, adhere to its principles. Even today's set designers and lighting technicians seem more interested in creating a believable and realistic effect than in creating spectacular but depthless results.

And yet, people, actors in particular, often ask why there is a need for the Method or, for that matter, any method. They seem to think that an actor should be empowered with a special native ability that sets him apart from other members of the human race, and which will automatically produce whatever emotion, characterization, movement, or truthful action that is called for in the script, performance after performance. Fortunately, this is not the case. I say fortunately when actually it would certainly be a wonderful convenience for the actor to possess, but at the same time would class actors as freaks of nature and remove them from the rank of creative artists. Therefore, there had to be a system developed artistically that would produce creatively those qualities which the actor desires in his interpretation of a role; a system that would produce them truthfully, not just on the surface with the voice and perfunctory gesture. Stanislavsky invented such a way.

When it is clearly understood that the Method is only a path, a means of discovering truth and honesty and then being able to apply it, the need for a method will be equally comprehensible.

It must not be thought (as it is by some), that the Method is intended to be a charismatic djin which will turn anyone into a great actor. One cannot depend upon the Method alone to achieve the ultimate in his art, for the actor must certainly possess the qualities in his soul that are inherent in all art. He must have sensitivity, awareness, both self and cosmogonal, good concentration, taste, temperament, intelligence, perseverance, and, lastly, the ability to communicate these qualities to the audience. The ability to communicate also holds true in relating to the other actors on stage. It is true that many of these qualities can be developed to some degree by the Method, but they must initially be present in the actor's make-up as a creative artist. The Method then should be used as an expediency, as a direct means to stimulate the growth of these qualities, to expand and embrace and encourage reality in the actor's work.

A student of Method acting does not receive a degree in his studies after a set length of time (a degree which says he has completed a certain number of hours of work, that he is now an actor who has learned his trade and is now ready to work). There is no set time which states when the actor's "instrument" is ready for practical use. Acting schools that have a semester system and graduation diplomas are usually very good examples of disloyalty to artistic creativity and aestheticism. Some phases of the Method can be grasped almost immediately and readily applied while other phases may involve problems of a personal nature and may take several years of training and study to resolve. It clearly depends on the individual. Over-all, however, it should be taken for granted that the Stanislavsky method of acting involves a lifetime of work and study. Life's experiences constantly change for everyone; nothing remains static and the true artist never stops trying to perfect his art. He never ceases to be curious about life and is constantly searching and adding, discarding and learning, and improving his technique.

It is far better for the young actor to work professionally at acting while he is studying the Method than to devote all his time to theoretic study alone. In this way, he can make the proper adjustments within himself and his instrument which are demanded by Method work to fully understand it and be able to put it to use.

Returning to the subject of a need for the Method in modern theatre, it must not be assumed that the Method itself is an inflexible device that can never change or that all of its rules can never experience any deviation. This book will show how in some instances it has already changed considerably since Stanislavsky's time and will continue to change according to outside forces whenever necessary. It is this exact need, dictated by outside forces, that brings about change and this in itself keeps the Method alive. If it were not flexible, it would have died in Stanislavsky's own time.

The outside forces which sometimes govern a change in

the Methods are as varied as our own society; for even our social needs and social evolvement can influence it greatly. Political changes which stress the kind of theatre that is to be presented to the people will also alter the Method. Economic conditions in the theatre itself (such as producers' timetables) can affect it and, of course, even actors are constantly changing it to suit their own artistic development as well as their own personal confines and limitations.

It is, I think, very important for every actor to realize that the sole purpose of the Method is not the *use* of the Method per se as has all too often become the case in the past few years. Many times we hear it said, "He's a Method actor" or "She uses the Method." Nobody ever seems to ask *how* one uses the Method. *How* and *why* it is used should be the main objective for the actor. Too often we get the feeling that the Method is using the actor instead of the reverse. It must never become anything except a procedure, an expedient road for each actor to find his own way toward ultimate truth in his art.

I have heard many actors who are known to be biased against the Method say, when learning more about it, that they had been using a certain phase of it for years without even knowing it. This may be true. However, whether they have done it consistently is at best conjecture. Learning to be consistent in using the Method is another matter entirely.

We have all heard it said by some actors at one time or another that acting should not be a conscious striving for reality; that acting is really just play, an imitation of life, a sham, pretense and hokum. These are the most disillusioned of all, for acting can never be any of these if it is to be considered an art form and its devotees are to be called artists.

Another outside force which affects the Method has to do with the amount of time granted for the preparation of a production. Whenever proper rehearsal time is lacking, the actual preparation of a role should take precedence over other aspects of the production. If the actors are Method actors it is easy to see how such an atmosphere would change certain facets of it. The basic tenets of it will never be destroyed by this or similar situations, but many of the varied phases and improvisational techniques that often lend conviction to a role and a feeling of security to the actor have to be eliminated, simply because of the time element in rehearsal.

It is a sad affair that the majority of plays produced in this country are under-rehearsed. It is an even sadder state that exists when most of our actors do not even realize this. They are so conditioned to accept the idea of a play being presented to the public after only four weeks of rehearsals that they almost always blame themselves for their lack of interpretation into a character. Plays more often than not arrive before the public with the actors feeling insecure in their parts due to under-rehearsal, or in a mental rut due to lack of feeling free in their characterizations. This feeling manifests itself by an impression that no aspect of the voice, movement, or character-thought can be permuted. It is an apathetic sensation akin to the cessation of life; that is, stage life. The latter comes from the rush to get the play ready, resulting usually in only one definite side of the character being portrayed. When this happens, quality is surely absent, to say nothing of the cramped feeling the actor suffers as an artist. Much of this is due to finances and the general economic problems of the producer. Consequently, the production and the art of the theatre are also affected. Much of this can be overcome by a thorough working knowledge of the Method, of where corners can be cut to attain almost the same high quality that can be derived from a full and relaxed rehearsal schedule. However, this does not mean that the problems which can affect the quality of the American theatre should be overlooked and condoned. The possibilities of the American theatre are absolutely limitless and yet, as it exists today, it is suffering from the doldrums and the degradation which arise from the greed of the businessmen who control it. The art of the theatre, and even its future, is negligible to such individuals and therefore suffers because of them. This one evil has existed in the American theatre since its conception. Only when the Federal Theatre Project was instituted did hope arise to erase this evil. But it failed and its downfall was due in part to a kind of greediness, a desire for complete artistic and political control.

There are many Russians today who complain that the Moscow Art Theatre has succumbed to some of the same destructive influences which Stanislavsky sought to destroy in the Russian theatre when he helped to found that brilliant assemblage of ensemble actors. It is said that much of the acting has become very mannered and conventional. It is also said that a certain "Moscow Art Theatre Style" has evolved that is unchanging from play to play and lacks even the color, vivacity, and excitement which the venerable Comedie Francaise offers through brilliant costumers, set designers, and a period style of superficial acting that is known for its conventionality. Another fault found with the Moscow Art Theatre is that the game of "theatre politics" is often played. Seniority often takes precedence resulting in actors of an advanced age portraying roles obviously too young for them.

Most of these reports come from the new "angry young men" of Russia who are somewhat on the order of our own young firebrand artists, desirous of change and tired of the old order of things. However, the degree of their contempt astonishes me. Many of them actually despise the Moscow Art Theatre. Going on the premise that the Moscow Art Theatre has come to this regrettable state, either through maladministration or lack of artistic foresight in properly continuing Stanislavsky's System, it would then seem obvious that the search for reality in the theatre and the adherence to the precepts of the original Moscow Art Theatre as set forth by Nemirovich-Danchenko and Stanislavsky is more evident in parts of the Western theatre than it is in Russia today. In such a case, it is easy to see that an important canon of Stanislavsky's method, *flexibility*, is being violated.

Even though modern Russia is very mindful of the need for cultural development for its citizens, it is also possible that the strictness of its political control does immeasurable harm to this development. It is the rare Russian today who will turn his back on social aspects and political realities in order to devote himself entirely to the cultivation of pure art. Too often the Russian artist, whether he be painter, musician, writer, sculptor, or actor, will let the state influence his art so that it contains a degree of propaganda, satire, indictment, or protest useful to the state. A pure art form can never exist under these conditions.

So, again in the field of acting we see how a system of acting which desires only the search for truth can be predisposed, unless its flexibility can be maintained. The Method, as it has come to us, is very flexible if permitted to be and is a system whereby all the precepts of a pure art form can be utilized. This is why there has to be a "method" for actors, actors everywhere. Only when the contrasting beauty and grace of the new, the fresh, and the real with hackneyed tradition is made obvious to the people will taste for the former and disdain for the latter begin to show. This change has already begun to such a degree that in our time we may very well see the end of certain decadent styles of acting that have damaged not only our art, but have even demeaned the public image of the actor throughout history.

The chapters that follow are meant to be as fundamentally intrinsic, graphic, and as basic as possible with regard to the Method. It is hoped that they will be read more than once by the serious student of acting.

The exercises in particular should be studied, worked on over and over, as often as possible. Other chapters dealing with mental or "inner" concentration, "inner" problems of the actor, and relaxation should be referred to liberally. The actor should find himself returning to the remaining portions of this book from time to time, depending upon his own progress.

It is also hoped that the reader, upon completion of this book, will find manifest the successful transference of Stanislavsky's Method from the Eastern theatre to the Western theatre and, if an actor, will be inspired to follow the path of genius that was Stanislavsky's.

On the Art of Acting

What is acting? Why is acting classified as an art form?

To begin with, true acting depends upon one main principle which ascertains its artistry: *whether or not it is real*. This principle is in turn related directly to the true definition of acting. If the above corollary seems slightly cryptic, let me clarify it by relating an incident that took place at a memorable occasion in my life.

On March 1, 1954, Lee Strasberg started a new series of private acting classes in addition to two other sets of classes previously formed. I enrolled in a private acting class and at this writing am still there.

Two hitherto unknown actresses began their studies there and, on that very first day of class, demonstrated quite graphically for the rest of the class exactly what acting as a definition should encompass.

The class began, as all new classes begin, with the usual type of friendly conversation intended to familiarize the students with each other and with their new teacher. Eventually the conversation turned to the inevitable: Acting, its definition, what it means. The students wanted Lee to set forth a definite verbalization, a clear-cut explanation of the term "acting."

Instead, he called upon the two young actresses to mount the stage in the classroom. One was Inger Stevens who had arrived in New York as Inger Stensland from Sweden by way of Lubbock, Texas, where her father was a college professor;

the other was Carroll Baker who had not too long before been traveling the country as a magician's assistant on the old and venerable Keith Circuit. Both had the idealistic fervor of youth regarding the theatre which would help propel them to the heights of stardom they presently enjoy.

Strasberg's instructions to the pair were simple and direct. Now that they were on the stage, all he wanted them to do was to begin acting for the rest of us! Amid protests that they had not prepared anything, much less together since they had not laid eye on each other before that day, Strasberg was adamant. "Act," he instructed, not bothering to suppress a smile. The protests began again as the two actresses bewailed their lack of material and asked how could they be expected to act without any preparation. Lee's direction this time was a little more enlightening to the class as well as to the hapless pair on stage and gave the necessary straw for support.

"What is the reality of your present situation?

"Of course you have not prepared anything for us. I didn't ask you to prepare anything and would not have wanted you to do so in the first place.

"Again I ask, What is the reality of your situation right at this very moment? This is the only thing you could possibly act for us. So do it. Act!"

After a rather stumbling beginning a small flicker of realization dawned in all our eyes as Inger and Carroll began to ask questions, real questions to and about each other. They asked each other their names, their whereabouts, past experience in the theatre, they expressed their hopes, desires, likes and dislikes until finally they were almost totally engrossed in their conversing and seemed relaxed and oblivious to the presence of Lee and the class. After fifteen minutes of this Lee interrupted the little scene, and equally engrossed class, by stating that what had taken place was true acting, pure in every sense, and that enough had been seen to determine a definition of acting.

"What you have just seen," said Strasberg, "is an example of truthful, believable acting. You have two human beings on a stage behaving exactly as they would in their own living room on being introduced, slightly reticent at first, then gradually warming to each other through their obviously real conversation. Therefore it is safe to assume that a good practical definition of acting would be this: *The ability to create complete reality while on a stage.*"

Now, the class immediately recognized the scene between Inger and Carroll to be *real* conversation concerning *actual* topics, answering *real* questions with *genuine* answers about their *real* selves. They, therefore, believed everything they heard and saw because they knew it to be true.

But now hands began to raise for recognition as expletives came to the effect that a real conversation with all its natural behavior is a far cry from one developed from an author's imagination: one that is made up of unfamiliar situations, alien words, foreign interpretations, unaccustomed movement and behavior.

"This," said Strasberg, "is why acting is an art. For it is when we are able to create reality, truth, and beauty out of such seemingly adverse conditions, out of a void so to speak, and to do it with just the basic implements of life around us, with just ourselves and nothing else to work with, then and only then, have we transformed the theatre and its works into an art form."

He continued with, "The purpose of these classes, and all future classes, is to train your instruments to be able to create that reality which was already present in the scene you just witnessed. When this is done the situations, all the involvements including plot, emotions, dialogue which the author has created, will be no less authentic to you than this scene was for Inger and Carroll."

So, then as now, this definition of acting remains constant. Acting is not pretending. It is not imitating or merely impersonating or pantomime or any of a hundred different names wrongly used to explain it. We know the one element that never fails to excite an audience, never fails to completely absorb them in the play they are watching, is that which they see around them in life and know to be true. It is when the audience can feel what the actors are feeling, experience what they experience, recognize the love, anguish, desire, hatred, or jealousy of the actor's role, that they become aware of the actor's art. It is this art, the art of achieving reality, real tears, real laughter, real expression, movement and voice, that will comprise this book.

The term "instrument" is used by nearly all Method actors. For those not familiar with it, I believe it wise to clarify it now since it is used quite extensively throughout this book.

An actor's instrument is his whole self. It is his body, his mind and being, complete with thoughts, emotions, sensitivity, imagination, honesty, and awareness. More will be said later concerning its functions and subsequent training, but for now try to imagine the actor's instrument in much the same way you picture the musician and his violin, the artist and his canvas, paints, and brushes. Think of them as one and inseparable. Just as the musician practices daily on his instrument, always perfecting its response to his will through training, and the artist mixes his paints, brushing them on with the precision and beauty accrued only by drill, so must the actor be concerned with the training and development of his instrument and its responses to his commands.

There is a vast difference between the art of living one's part and merely representing or playing it. An actor must create a living human being on stage with all the complexities of the character: his behavior, thoughts, emotions and their subsequent transitions. He must never settle for less. It is indeed a tragedy that there is such a dearth of art inherent in all the many media of theatre today. This is not to say that one should necessarily live an "art for art's sake" existence, though to some true artists this seems reason aplenty and would seem quite refreshing amidst the hackneyed "art" which threatens to ruin at least one acting medium of today.

Because of economic necessity, it is often difficult to bring together in an ensemble of theatrical art, all of the artistry of the individual actor. Again, the demand of the producer's timetable for this artistry to be complete, especially in the Western theatre, is practically a negation of the art of acting with which the other creative arts are seldom hampered. The painter can paint until he alone is artistically satisfied; the musician and composer can work until their music is a part of them before scheduling a concert; the writer-author may write and rewrite over a period of years before he is satisfied. The actor, however, is more or less trapped in a Seine of time schedules centered around rehearsals in which he has to consciously create his art *on time*. This is just one of many annoyances that pique our artistic sensibilities, but at the same time it lends credibility to the need for training our instruments in the ways of truth as opposed to technique understood as accomplishment.

Unlike other professions where an eight-hour day is deemed the normal amount of time to be devoted, acting requires a constant adherence to the profession itself. The actor's day should begin long before he reaches the theatre for the evening's performance. Whether he is working on a role or not, his day should begin as an actor when he awakens. Whether it be personal introspection, surveillance of life around him, appreciation of nature and her laws, awareness of people and their problems, or trying to wake up in the morning as the character he is playing, the actor must continually strive for perceptivity. For by seeing deeper than the surface aspects of life, he is able to broaden his own scope of any character he portrays. The depth of his art will depend greatly upon this perceptiveness. This will be shown to a larger degree later on in the book.

The pursuance of any artist's endeavor always involves periods of transition for the artist until he can chart the clear course of direction that his artistic sensibilities demand. For this reason I believe it necessary to rise in defense of a situation that, while admittedly lamentable, is often temporary and certainly understandable.

It is sometimes maliciously stated that students of the Method do not pay attention to their own voice or speech problems, that they mumble, often purposely, and that they move on stage as though they were being subjected to a series of limbering-up exercises. If these critics stated that *some* students of the Method acted this way, their statements would perhaps have some measure of truth. Unfortunately, it is always the Method and its training that takes the brunt of the blame. The complaints registered against it are true only to the extent of certain actors' emotional problems which are, regrettably, manifested on stage. What these critics do not realize is that the training of an actor's instrument to respond truthfully is contrary to the artificial laws of society. We know that much of what is deemed ''correct'' and ''proper'' in our society is a complete refutation of nature's laws. We also know that this refutation begins in childhood when we have little control over its effect. More will be said later about the natural conflict with rules dictated by social convention.

In the case of the actor who has been trained in a different school of acting than that of the Method, and who wants to change over entirely to a more realistic kind of acting, the problems involved in destroying the bad habits he has learned make the task doubly hard.

Many actors who are not satisfied with the false superficiality of their performances, due to earlier training, are turning in ever increasing numbers to teachers who are advocates of Stanislavsky. Most of what they have learned from previous teachers must be eliminated. Tearing down what they have learned and then rebuilding and retraining their instruments is hard not only on the teacher but also on the student.

It is entirely probable that many actors have been seen in performances while in the throes of a particularly difficult transitional period of their studies, and, due to some particular problem, their work was affected by it. The critic may then ask why the actor does not finish his study and training before he tries acting. If he did this, he would probably never act because the actual performing of his art is necessary for his development. Also, his training and learning never really end. He must devote his whole life to knowing just a little bit more, day by day. *There is no beginning and no end to learning.*

Work on one's self, which our method stresses so emphatically, is the most formidable task for an artist. So, in answer to those detractors who are not familiar with our method and quite possibly not familiar with all those who apply it, as there have always been imitators and coattail grabbers, let me say in truth that the Method actor is very much aware of speech, natural movement in harmony with his voice, thoughts, and emotions. These are all the results of the instrument he is eagerly training for use on the stage and often, too, his development as a human being.

Furthermore, he is brave enough as well as perceptive enough to portray a play's character as it really should be portrayed, as the author intended it to be portrayed. This has been demonstrated in this country by the best performances of the last thirty-five years. The chapters which follow, with the emphasis on the exercises designed to train the instrument, will add verification to the Method actor's dedication to that which represents truth. This truth can only come from the actor himself through his training. There is no greater joy for any actor than when he can, through long and sometimes arduous self-exploration, find new qualities of his own individuality which will in turn apply to the character he is portraying. He is seldom content and is constantly searching to improve his performances with truthful and exciting expressiveness. This is often a difficult task to accomplish due sometimes to our standards of conventional social behavior.

This behavior is evident in nearly everything we do and is first started in our childhood. It is not a natural manifestation. It is, instead, instilled and enforced, usually unwittingly, by well-meaning parents. Many theorists believe this to be the reason why the average actor experiences extreme difficulty in bringing onto the stage that which an ordinary human being feels and thinks every day of his life. Because most of us have all our lives been taught to suppress many of our natural feelings, instincts, and emotions from childhood to adulthood, we are now faced with the issue of expressing them as actors to an audience while still unable to express them in our own lives. This is indeed a problem that forces the teacher to emphasize to the student the need for honest expression in his personal relationship with life before he can expect to come to terms with a particular role.

Quite obviously the answer to the problem as a whole must come from the proper attitude of adult to child, child to adult. The relationship with children should be one of cooperative understanding if none of the child's emotional outlets are to be stifled or, perhaps worse, shifted to an unreal direction.

When a child falls down and scrapes his knee, how many times have we heard an adult try to halt the tears with the admonition, "Stop crying. Big boys don't cry. It isn't the manly thing to do." Obviously not. If he were a man he probably would not cry but instead curse his head off. I wonder which is worse? Who would be adhering closer to nature's laws, the man or the little boy? How many times have young girls been told by anxious mothers not to laugh so loud because it isn't the "ladylike" way to behave? I know more than one actress who has had difficulty in a role where the character was supposed to laugh heartily, simply because she had been taught it was wrong to laugh that way.

Unfortunately, this situation exists in other art forms besides acting. The child who shows a desire to draw or paint is often subjected to ridicule because his art "does not look like a tree." This does not come from other children but from adults, sometimes even his "teacher." Of course, his attempts at drawing or painting might have looked like a tree to the young artist, but because he wants to escape further ridicule, he condescends to draw the tree's trunk and branches like everyone else's. Probably subconsciously he realizes something is amiss, but he is too young to cope with "authority." It is usually only a matter of time before he discards his pencils and paints for something else, his earliest form of artistic expression destroyed in its infancy.

These are but a few of the myriad instances of repression that society has placed upon us since childhood. It is deplorable at best. For any artist to be free to express his art with truth, these repressions must always be torn away and replaced with the ability to vent, if necessary, honest and open-faced expressions and emotions.

Children should be treated not only as children but as equal human beings. They should also be treated as masters in their own way. Can the freshness, the originality, and the honesty of a child in the midst of describing a thing wondrous to him be duplicated or denied by any adult? How can any so-called grown-up person justify stifling the candid frankness and innocent openheartedness of a child by subtly, or outwardly, repressing him? This is the beginning of his repression, caused by his forced adherence to inhibiting and unnatural rules. It is a natural thing to weep when we are sad or when we have been hurt. It is natural to laugh loudly when we are happy. It is also natural to vent temper when we are angry. But these emotions have become so involved and twisted by the time a child grows to maturity that they are hardly recognizable.

Children live to a great extent with emotions based on fact and truth of feeling. A child expresses himself in response to inner motivations. Everything he does in play, or in seriousness, is a result of these motivations. They are easy, natural, honest, just. But when the adult decides to impose his will and dominate these motivations with his established conventions, the easy naturalness gives way and so does the child's inherent aestheticism. Then begins the long road of typical adult restraint and repression which, if he later chooses a life in art, must eventually be destroyed. Oddly enough, this process is often the reason for some people turning toward the arts; as a means of finding self-expression that was deprived them earlier in life.

One would be surprised at the number of stutterers and tone deaf actors present in the theatre today due to childhood suppression of their emotions. Is it any reason to wonder that many actors have to devote years to retrain and correct an inadequacy drilled into them all their lives?

We can all learn important lessons from children. They are totally unaware of being blessed with natural self-expression when very young, and this is a state to which every actor should aspire. He must strive for a freedom and openness in his art that is not forced; one that is inspired by his awareness, but motivated by his need to reject all that is fake, pretentious, and untrue to life.

Oddly enough, the healthy qualities intrinsic to human beings in childhood that would allow them greater freedom as artists later in life but are usually smothered by that time, are seen consistently in all animals that have resisted domestication and are ruled by instinctive natural laws. There are many acting exercises involving the study of animals, discussed later in this book, that are of infinite benefit to the development and response of the actor's instrument.

My belief that cats are pretty good actors is well-founded. The cat is a household pet that has resisted domestication by man throughout the ages. True, they are tame, will purr and rub against you for affection, come to be fed, play, and behave generally like any other domesticated animal—with one exception—they will do this only if they want to. No amount of coaxing, training, or spanking will make cats obey if they deem otherwise. They are completely independent by nature. They have many of the qualities, good and bad, that actors have. They are lithe, graceful, selfish, and vain. They possess excellent concentration, are perfect imitators of their larger and more ferocious cousins, have a spirited imagination, and possess the ability to bring all of these characteristics into perfect play.

If you have ever watched a cat stalk a live mouse, you saw there was no difference in his approach when he is playing with a toy mouse, a cotton ball, or a piece of crinkly paper. His mind is completely free from outside distractions while concentrating on the object. Nothing else but the object is important. He will stalk the imagined quarry, strike at it in mock battle, dodge, flee in terror and hide, only to wait for the propitious time to pounce again. But do not ever think that he really believes the object to be a real mouse, for after a while he will lose interest in it and just as quickly as he started to play, he will drop it.

The important note of interest for the actor is that whatever the cat imagines the piece of string or toy mouse to be is immediately expressed with his whole body by assuming the physical and mental attitudes of the hunt or the battle. When a cat plays at hunting, his keen imitative ability closely approaches art.

The principle of force of truth in a cat's actions is, at the same time, the most essential ingredient to the art of acting. However, no art is truly complete unless it reaches the people and nourishes and sustains them. It cannot stand alone. Actors are too inclined to brood about their art instead of realizing the immense pleasure to be gained from it. They hardly seem to realize that their art is being expressed literally with their own sweat and blood. It is an actor's voice, his face, his hands, his blood that produces the art seen by the audience. What a resplendent tribute this is to his craft, to his person, to his very soul. His art rewards him with this glorification and at the same time serves to enlighten mankind to the heights of awareness. The emotional power capable of being transmitted to the beholder should always have enlightenment as its purpose. Prejudices and illiberalities can be eliminated through the theatre's power of truth and conviction. Actors must perceive this and find meaning in their potential to serve mankind.

Also, the actor must find personal delight from his profession. One seldom hears an actor speak of the unalloyed pleasure he feels while acting. Actors should not be afraid to admit that acting is not only a delight and pure joy but also a great deal of fun. It is and we all know it is, but for some reason we are ashamed to admit it. We should be both proud and glad that we can attain this from our art.

The following chapter begins the discussion of the actual components of the Method as it has been passed on to us from the great Stanislavsky. There have been alterations in the system taught by him; some slight, some more than minor, and some aspects of his system have been discarded altogether due to impracticality. This impracticality is in turn due to the differences, social, economic, and cultural, which govern the artistic sensibilities of the individual as well as the group.

However, the most important changes in the system have been ones that the master himself would have approved of.

They are the advancements of his ideas in his system that have been made in the Western theatre; advancements and adjustments that are definitely needed if Stanislavsky's system was to become a method of finding truth in the theatres of the Western world.

In the chapters that follow, a more than cursory analysis of the components that comprise the Method will be explained. This will be done largely by the use of analogies. It is hoped, too, that the components of the Method will reveal to the reader why the Method is not just a theory, but a practicable art. Art is best created without a theory.

*"In the name of God, stop a
moment, cease your work,
look around you."*
    Tolstoy

Sense Memory

Sense Memory is the most vital component of the Method.
It is also the most controversial among certain teachers who
profess to teach Stanislavsky's System. Many teachers prefer
to eliminate this all-important part of training for their own
various reasons. Undoubtedly, the real reason lies in their
own ineptness to comprehend its importance. Without it, it
is impossible to create the stimulus that sets off that reaction
to objects on stage in a way that is real and believable.

The reader will discover in the following chapters, as he
goes from one phase of the Method to the other, that a foundation of Sense Memory is present in every phase. This foundation must be built before the actor can progress further.
Even the most difficult exercises have Sense Memory as their
basis, and the most difficult acting problems can usually be
solved by a complete understanding of it.

Sense Memory is exactly what the name implies. It is a
remembering of the five senses: sight, sound, touch, taste,
smell. The use of Sense Memory brings a feeling of life to
every object that is associated with these five senses.

Now the young actor may say, but there is nothing wrong
with my hearing, or my eyesight and, for that matter, nothing
ails any of my senses. Why should I trouble myself with
learning to make my senses remember when they now function fine?

This is all true. An actor's senses may function as they
should in life, but do they behave as they should on stage?

When you pick up an object on stage, is that object as real to you as it would be in life? Probably not. The reason for this is that we cannot just say to ourselves that we will experience a sensory sensation in a certain scene and then expect it to appear. It is not that easy. If acting were all that simple, we would have nothing but truth presented on our stages, whereas we know that a really truthful expression of feeling is a great moment of beauty only too rare on stage. An actor, just because the author wills it, cannot call upon himself to experience the pains of a serious disease or injury simply by saying, as if by magic, "I have a pain here"—"or there." No, that pain has to be created, worked for, practiced in a detailed series until he can then recall it at will. In this chapter, these steps will be produced in some detail for the reader in a manner that will train his senses to react to the imagined stimuli, thus awakening the proper sensory response.

I must be peremptory in stressing the importance, to the actor, of complete comprehension of this initial foundation of the Method before trying to understand the chapters which follow.

In this chapter, I shall show how Sense Memory is almost a sense in itself, one that has to be developed; that it is very difficult while on stage to display the five senses in their true perspective and also to give an understanding of Sense Memory in order to lay the groundwork for nearly every other part of the Method. Again, I repeat, Sense Memory is the basic foundation upon which Stanislavsky built his system. To eliminate it from acting or teaching is to attempt to build a skyscraper on air, without steel, concrete, or earth to support it.

To begin with, I must stress that an actor's awareness is of prime importance in accomplishing the tasks of Sense Memory's application. He should realize that the human body is his instrument just as much as the violin is an instrument of a musician, or the paint and canvas is the instrument of the painter. Through his body, his sensitivity, emotions, and intellect, the actor produces his art. The musician, through practice, familiarizes himself with every vibration, every tone, and every chord that his instrument can produce as well as its limitations. The painter knows grades of canvas, the quality of brushes, and how to blend his paints into the beautiful and reassuring mirror of his pictures. So it must be with the actor. He must study nature's laws of the physical life and those reactions which motivate and affect his instrument, his sensations, and his emotions.

The basis will be given in a series of exercises that can be practiced in the privacy of one's own room. Even if they are inculcated in class work, they should be practiced in private, over and over again, ever widening the variety of the exercises, and done every day as faithfully as a musician practices his scales.

One real sensation at the beginning of a scene can give the needed impetus to whatever the desired affect, and when one reality is created it is easier to go into another, and then another, and still another, until real situations develop and the play takes on a positive sense of credibility. All great moments in life are composed of smaller moments. The same applies on the stage, and it is these small moments that we will concern ourselves with in this chapter.

For instance, in a play, valuable jewelry is duplicated in glass or other valueless materials. But how many times have we seen an actor pick up an object supposedly worth thousands of dollars, according to the story-line of the script, and treat it like its actual worth, maybe a few paltry dollars. On the other hand, he may realize that the object's worth should be ''played,'' and then indicate this to the audience with the same falseness of feeling so that we who are watching him do not believe either of his ''playings.'' Incidentally, I use the word ''play'' in the literal sense, for it certainly is not acting.

There should be no set pattern as to how a valuable object should be treated, as that is left to the individual actor's imagination, but in life a person will not pick up, look at, and treat a bracelet studded with diamonds *exactly* the same way he would pick up a piece of worthless junk. It is, therefore, up to the actor to create for himself a real value for the worthless object.

So often we see an actor in the theatre or movies drinking what is supposed to be, say—straight whiskey. He may be playing the leading role of the virile, strong man and consequently we see him throwing down drink after drink with hardly a bat of the eyelashes. In other words, he drinks it as if it were what it actually is, colored water, tea, or some other mild beverage which the prop-man has provided. The average audience, so accustomed to seeing such hero-feats as this, will say, if questioned about his lack of believability, "Well, do you expect him to drink *real* whiskey?" The answer to this is, of course, no, as then he would not be acting. But was he acting when he did not bother to create "real" whiskey for us through his actor's talent? Obviously not. How much better it would have been for him to be able to set for himself simple sensory tasks that would create for the audience a sense of reality in his performance.

Suppose he had first tried to remember the smell of whiskey, as he brought the glass to his lips. Then suppose he had tried to remember how the alcohol feels when it first touches the lips, enters into the mouth, and flows around the inside of the lips, around the tongue, to the back of the mouth. Then, the all-important swallow. There is a sense of whiskey being all on its own as it starts its trek downward. Do not forget that whiskey burns when taken "straight," and in life one never drinks whiskey the exact same way one would drink tea or water. Therefore, the process does not end with the swallow. There may be some residue left in the mouth and, if so, still some taste. There may also be a continuation of the stinging of the alcohol. There is not a standard result from these few tasks as each actor must use himself to determine what the results are. But if the actor had first taken the time to do these tasks and follow them through to their logical conclusions, then we would believe him when he shows the first signs of intoxication. All of these tasks precede the effects of the alcohol.

You may wonder how to make your senses remember.

They cannot be forced. However, they will work just as naturally and easily on stage as in life if you supply the little
amount of concentration and practice that is needed.

To give you a simple illustration of how our senses work
in life, without our ever being aware of it, take the situation
of going to your own closet in the dark. We have all done
that at some time or another. You do not even bother to turn
on the lights but just reach your hand inside the closet, lightly
brushing the articles of clothing with your fingers, and pull
out the coat or sweater you are seeking without actually seeing the object. Yet, you did ''see'' it with your fingers as
soon as they touched it.

In life, one's senses remember all by themselves. On stage,
they have to be trained consciously to function as they do in
life. Also, they will never get to the point of functioning by
themselves on stage without conscious effort being applied
at *every* performance. This means that every night on stage,
this effort, the setting of certain tasks and then following
them through, must be repeated faithfully. This is true, not
only with regard to Sense Memory but, also, in respect to
every phase of the Method. The reason for this is that once
the desired results of the scene have been decided upon by
the director, they will be consistently done in every performance.

The exercises given will only be several of literally hundreds that can be added through everyday experience. The
''objects'' in the exercises will be strictly imaginary and of
the actor's own choosing. If inculcated into class work, they
can be judged only by someone who knows what to look for
in his criticism.

Without using the actual object, you may practice any
number of things you do every day. Drinking a cup of coffee,
a cup of tea, combing your hair, tying your shoes, or sitting
in the sun, are just a few to choose from. You may examine
the actual object first to test it for texture, weight, balance,
etc. Then begin the exercise without the object. One very
important aspect of doing any of these exercises is that the
actor does not concern himself with facial reactions at all.

Do not try to "show" what an object looks like, how it feels, or how it tastes. This is where the actor's awareness of what he is doing is most important. In life, when drinking a cup of hot coffee, you do not try to show the coffee is hot. The coffee *is* hot, your senses know it, they react to it without your conscious awareness, and anyone watching you drink the coffee will know it is hot.

In other words, if the actor's concentration is concerned with creating the sense he is working for, the sense will make the face react of its own accord in the simple and natural way it does in life. The audience will see this in exactly the same way it would if you were being observed off-stage doing the same everyday thing.

To begin work on any of the following exercises, it is most important to relax. This is particularly true if applied in a class with other actors. I shall take up the subject of tension and relaxation in a subsequent chapter, but for now, we shall strive for simple muscular relaxation.

First, pick a straight-back chair without armrests or up-holstery and try to get into a comfortable sitting position whereby, *if you had to do so, you could fall asleep.* Relax the arms, shoulders, and all places of obvious tension including the back of the neck, around the eyes, temples, and mouth.

The first object to work for will be the aforementioned cup of coffee. I shall try to guide the thinking process of the reader in these first exercises so as to prod his actor's awareness to the object he is trying to create. Remember, too, concentration on the "object" is of paramount importance and pantomimic gestures are not to be used at all.

EXERCISE I

(A) Try to see before you, on an imaginary table, the cup you wish to create for yourself. Trace the outlines of it letting your eyes fall on each part of it from the top down to the handle, down to the bottom, and back up the other side. Focus your eyes on the exact location where you wish the cup to be, for this aids concentration. Then, try to see the color and contour as a whole. These should come to you after one or two tries.

(B) Next, slowly reach out your hand and place the index finger through the imaginary cup handle. Gently lift the cup and while doing so, become aware, by remembering, of the shift in weight and balance as the cup is raised. The rest of the fingers and the hand play an important part in this stage. You will notice that in life a full cup is not lifted with one finger alone. The whole hand comes into play and, indeed, the whole arm and shoulder. Remember, too, that when any object is picked up, the thumb and index finger do not touch. In doing the exercise, you must leave room for the object, in this case, the handle, to fit inside the fingers. Try to judge the right amount of space between the fingers in any object you choose to pick up and consciously try to remember the texture, weight, and anything else that would occur if you were doing the same thing in real life.

(C) Now comes the crucial task of placing the hot coffee into the cup. In life we can close our eyes and tell if a cup is empty or full by feeling the shift in balance. The liquid will move from side to side as the cup is tilted. Try to feel where the liquid moves as it sloshes back and forth in the cup. Do this very slowly and gently. Remember that this exercise is not supposed to be a pantomimic gesture. It is only a training exercise used to awaken the actor's senses and should always be done very slowly.

(D) Can you now begin to feel the warmth of the liquid through the handle of the cup? Remember that in life you can almost tell if the coffee is too hot to drink by the temperature of the cup in your hand. Try to create for yourself the warmth of the cup, then slowly bring it toward your lips. As the cup gets about halfway between the imaginary table and your mouth, you should then begin to realize the first strong aroma of the coffee. Here you must just make the effort to work for the sense of smell. Do not worry about any facial reactions. Concern yourself only with carrying out the simple sensory tasks of the exercise.

(E) At about this point in the exercise, let me suggest that you become aware of any tension in the body. Consciously make the effort to relax. Do this while still holding the cup and carrying out the exercise. The "object," or cup, should be near the lips now, and the actor should try to trace with his eyes the outline of the top of the cup and the liquid in it. As the coffee comes to the lips, the "feeling" of heat from the liquid will be very strong around the area of the mouth and nose, if the exercise is working.

(F) In the last stage of the exercise, the actor should again be warned not to concern himself with any facial reactions. He should watch himself only for the express purpose of concentrating on the object that he is creating.

As the hand brings up the cup, try to see the edge of it and judge where the rim of it should be. This judging of distance is purely a technical task, done to aid the actor in the transition of one's senses.

Now try to feel the rim as it rests against the lips. Do not be afraid to experiment in order to create the object. If you are unable to "feel" the rim of the cup, gently run the tongue around the edge of the "rim" or bring the other hand into play and, gently with a finger, try to trace the rim. Nevertheless, do not force it, and if you do not succeed at first, pass by that phase of the exercise and proceed to the next.

(G) Tilt the cup toward the lips gently and slowly. Take just a "sip" of the "coffee," and concentrate on the sense of heat, the smell, and then, the taste. (Careful not to spill it.)

You should not be worried if at first you are unable to keep these three or four sensory sensations working at the same time. That will come with only three or four attempts at the exercise.

(H) The last step comes with the intake of the coffee. Is it sweet or bitter, does it have cream and sugar in it? You can decide these questions and answer them for yourself before you begin the exercise.

As the coffee enters the mouth, try to remember, along with the heat, taste, etc., exactly where it goes from there. A little goes around the inside of the lips, under the tongue, along the cheeks, over the tongue to the back of the mouth, and then down the throat. Is there any residue left on the lips after the swallow? We usually find ourselves swallowing more than once on just one sip, too. In life, the process does not even stop there. After reaching the stomach, there is a definite sensation of it being there. However, for now we shall just be concerned with creating the "cup of coffee" and not any theoretical continuations.

The same exercise can be practiced with a glass of milk, a cold drink, or any number of everyday practices which are familiar to all of us. The more variety the actor exposes himself to in these exercises, such as working for first a hot drink, then a cold one, the better his senses will become trained.

When working on sensory "objects" in an actors' class, the object being worked for should not be divulged until after the exercise is completed. The reason for this is to test the strength of the exercise and, also, to test the class reaction to it by asking the class to identify the "object." This invariably leads to a not always unanimous version, but it is valuable for several reasons. It tests the observations of the rest of the class and helps them to learn by watching others work. It also exhibits the varying facets of imagination inherent in all of us. Now, the actor who is doing the exercise should never worry if everyone did not recognize the object of his labor. I must repeat again that it is fatal to be concerned with showing the exercise. Even if it is not recognized immediately by the rest of the class *or* the teacher, there will be moments when everyone will be conscious that the senses were "working." This is the purpose of the exercise and the most important aspect of it. The actual exercise itself, at this moment, will become unimportant because the purpose of training the senses and the creation of the stimuli that breathe like of them is really what the actor is seeking, not the *performing* of the exercise.

For the second step, let us take an exercise that at first glance may seem to some a bit more simple than the first.

This will be strictly for the sensation of sunshine on the body. I shall refer to it, as I did the previous exercise, as "working for" sunshine. The creation of sunshine may seem to some as a somewhat abstract type of sensation. By this I mean there will be no coffee cup to "hang onto" or to touch, taste, or smell, as in the first exercise. However, anyone who has ever sat directly in the rays of a good hot sun, will realize there is nothing abstract about the experience.

Most of us will admit that sitting in the sun is a distinct pleasure because of the warmth and almost life-giving sensation it affords our bodies. To illustrate but one of the myriad subtle variations the actor will discover as he progresses with sensory exercises, take the supposition that an actor is very fair-skinned and actually dislikes the sun's rays because of what they do to him. The exercise would then transfer to the beholder the impression of a totally different type of exercise, possibly pain of some sort. This can have interesting results and can be used in various acting roles that call for that particular sensation as well as the normal reaction to the sun's rays. A few actors have difficulty in experiencing pain that is directly worked for, possibly hesitating to recall the experience to the conscious mind and, in such a case, an indirect method of creating the pain can be useful. We shall proceed on the premise that the actor has normal appreciation and regard for the sun and that its effect will be due to the fullness and strength of the exercise.

EXERCISE II

(A) Use the same kind of straight-back chair used in Exercise I, making the same effort to relax and to rid the body of all muscle tension. Put the body into a position in the chair whereby you could come the closest to falling asleep if need be. Sit in the chair in an attitude of basking in the sun. Most probably the eyes will be closed and the body motionless.
(B) Now try to make the effort to remember the sensation of the sun on your face. When you sit in the sun, where do you feel the heat of its rays on your face? Do not say that you feel them all over your face. Generally, this may be true, but not specifically. There are specific places where the sun is felt

first, and generalizations have no place whatsoever in sensory exercises. The first places on your face which experience the sensation of sunshine are the places most exposed. That is, the higher planes of the face; these being the bridge of the nose, the forehead, and perhaps the upper lip.

Keep your concentration centered on these locales and then gradually let your "sun" descend on the rest of the body.

(C) Try to remember how its rays feel as they soak into your clothing. Where do you feel the heat of the rays on your body? If you will notice, the feeling is slightly different when the rays hit a clothed area than when they hit the face. The rest of the body will feel a degree of heat ranging from a mild body warmth to a sticky, stifling kind of heat, depending upon the actor's concentration.

(D) Now go back to the face and, as you quietly sit in concentration, try to remember the feeling of the sun when you remain exposed to it for any prolonged length of time. Recall the sensation of heat-caused perspiration around the forehead, the moistness of the hair line, the minute beads of perspiration that form across the nose and under the eyes and on the chin. If your concentration is working on recalling all of these tasks and any more peculiar to the individual, you should now begin to experience a definite awakening of the senses involved. It usually takes only one or two attempts with full concentration to stimulate the senses to react in full force as they would under the actual conditions.

(E) Return again to the area of the body and the legs. With the legs stretched out in front of you, define *exactly* for yourself where you feel the sun strongest. (This will vary with the individual, too.) Become aware of the sensation of clothes clinging to the body during the heat of a midday sun.

(F) Concentrate now on the area of the body that is not exposed directly to the sun's rays (the back of the leg, the nape of the neck, under the arm, the seat, etc.) continuously exploring the sensations of one and then the other, finally returning again to the face. Spend at least fifteen minutes on the exercise, concentrating on and becoming aware of the various degrees and kinds of heat the body experiences. As soon as one degree or kind of heat is experienced, try to hold on to it and go to another. Do not be solicitous if on the first attempt you are unable to keep them all going at the same time. It sometimes requires several attempts, depending upon the individual actor's strength of concentration.

An exercise such as the previous one is supposed to result in a partial or complete reality depending on what the individual actor thinks is best for the scene in which he is using it. I have seen actors in class sit under the cold glare of a stage work light high above them with the perspiration flowing off their faces and leaving the telltale marks of dampness on their clothing.

At this point, I would like the reader to reflect upon the tremendous amount of realism which it is possible to bring to a scene by the accomplishment of these simple tasks. If a scene in a play calls for the sensory exercise just described, imagine how easily the author's words would flow through the reality of the actor's creation. A real sun is created without benefit of a sun being there. The author's lines are just as believable to the audience as if said in life, for the actor has created the reality of the situation out of which words are derived. This is just one phase of acting in its purest form.

For the third exercise we will work for pain, but it is not necessary to stay with the pain set down in the exercise. You can perhaps, find a pain that will be more clearly defined for your own individual senses. However, it is important *not* to recall a pain that has any psychological or emotional connection with it. That is another phase of the work which will be discussed in a subsequent chapter.

We will begin with a simple pain in the tooth. This is a problem most of us have experienced and one that is localized at first inspection to the area of the tooth itself.

EXERCISE III

(A) Begin the exercise in the same kind of chair used before. Apply the same technique for ridding the body of tension and take the necessary time to relax completely. Keep the eyes closed throughout the exercise in order to aid concentration.

There will be many questions that you can ask yourself as you proceed with the exercise.

What kind of pain is a toothache? Is it going to be a dull ache or a sharp pain? Pick the area in the mouth that you will concentrate on and remember the initial sensation of the toothache for which you are going to work.

(B) Try to recall exactly where in the tooth the pain begins. Does it hurt to touch the tongue to the afflicted tooth? The actor must ask himself many questions recalling the sensation of the pain and must keep his concentration on the (task) area. If the concentration begins to waver, put more effort toward relaxation and the tension problem.

(C) Now ask yourself if there is any heat or inflammation with the pain. Is the gum around the tooth sensitive to touch? Does cold air affect the pain in any way?

Take plenty of time with these initial tasks to be sure of getting a good foundation for the continuation of the exercise.

(D) Begin to recall if the rest of the teeth are in any way affected by the one bad tooth. Does the pain spread to them or to the jaw or to the upper part of the face?

Toothaches can manifest themselves in other associated little aches and pains of which we must be aware. Sometimes, the side of the face will hurt, the head will throb, or the back of the neck will ache, even extending as far as the back and shoulders.

(E) Again I say as I did in Exercises I and II, do not try to "show" that you are feeling pain. Just concentrate fully on the sensory tasks permitting any results to occur unconsciously as they do in life. In life we can tell when a person has a toothache; he does not have to tell us or gesticulate for us in order to know that there is something wrong. This is, of course, if he is genuinely feeling the pain. The difference here is that the actor will only be recalling or remembering the sensation and will not actually have the pain.

However, the result to the audience will be as if he were

experiencing the pain. A primary task is to train the actor's senses to react to the stimuli he creates through his imagination with the same degree of reality as in life.

(F) When the actor has explored all the possible variations of the exercise that he can remember, stop the exercise. Later, try to recall any phases of a toothache that you may have left out of this exercise. It would not hurt to make notes of any accompanying sensations to all the exercises practiced.

In Exercise II, I stated that the effects of sunshine may be different for each individual. The same is true of the exercise for pain or for any exercises you may do in the future. A very practical matter to keep in mind is that the audience never knows exactly what the actor is thinking. Therefore, after the actor discovers what results he obtains from certain exercises, he can fit the result, *not the exercise*, to the scene he is playing.

I have seen an actor "working for pain" in class, but the result was entirely something else to those watching. What the actor transmitted to the class as a whole was the impression of complete reverie, of being in a musing state of mind. Now this would not do if a scene called for a distinct and sharp pain. It would, however, most certainly be correct if the scene had called for a kind of tranquility in the character. So here we have the case of an actor using one specific type of exercise to lend a completely different "air" to his character in the scene than that which was expected.

The actor must experiment with all of these exercises and become aware of his senses and their reactions if he is to be able to pick and choose the correct one for application. This will serve the reader as an illustration of the extent to which the beginning actor must train his instrument.

It is easy for us to transmit, even in life, the wrong thoughts to others. How many times have we been thinking one thing and had someone misinterpret our thoughts? This is because we do not always express facially exactly what we are thinking. However, there usually is an expression there and this is where the actor has to know what the expression reveals to the bachelor. He should continually strive to penetrate into the most subtle expressions that he makes. This is where classwork and a perceptive teacher enter in; for he can guide the actor in informing himself of his various emotions, sensations, and mannerisms which are expressed facially. Under no circumstances should an actor try to uncover these expressions by use of a mirror. It is impossible for any human being to combine the practice of an exercise, the observation of it, and the objectivity needed to define it, all at the same time.

The actor must remember too that even though a person may misinterpret someone's thoughts in life, as well as on stage, the person will never deny having seen real thoughts going on. The same is true in acting if the actor's concentration is being applied. This is why practice on these exercises is so important. After his senses have been trained to the point where they will work easily when called upon, the actor can pick and file away mentally those he will need in the future. He should try constantly to add to his "repertoire" of exercises as he will find that they will enrich his own awareness of life around him and give source to his stage life. He will also find more insight into his instrument when he progresses to the stage of being able to combine two or more of his exercises concurrently: For example, carrying out completely Exercise I (the cup of coffee) while simultaneously carrying out Exercise II (sunshine). He will discover through his concentration that the coffee will take on an entirely different meaning "under the sun," so to speak.

This is not hard to realize. In real life our reactions are always motivated by outside forces of one kind or another. A person will not drink coffee in exactly the same way while sitting in an exclusive restaurant or while sitting in his own kitchen or while sitting in the sun. We are constantly affected by environmental differences, usually unconsciously. However, on stage, these differences do not exist and must be consciously created to follow the script line.

I suggest that before the actor tries to combine two distinct exercises, he first do one exercise which consists of two or more sensations involving the same sense. A good example of this would be to taste a piece of candy, and then a piece of lemon. The exercise will involve only the sense of taste, but two different "senses" of the sense of taste. Another exercise is the touch of three different kinds of material, all involving only the sense of touch. Make the materials as different from each other as possible; such as wool, chiffon, or perhaps a coarse fur. When these exercises are successfully done, which they should be in no more than three or four tries for each, the actor is then ready to proceed full steam ahead in developing his sensory training to its fullest. This will include more difficult sensory exercises such as showering, brushing the teeth, tying shoe laces, standing in the rain, applying lipstick, putting on hose, and the more advanced senses of pain.

He should now be able to make up his own exercise with relative ease. It is not necessary to include in this chapter exercises for the senses of sight and sound because the previous exercises should give enough insight into their performance. Sound (or listening exercise, as it is sometimes called) includes any sounds which are common and familiar to the individual. Music is very good for this exercise. The sense of sight can be done in an exercise by simply trying to recreate a scene in front of you which is very familiar; one in which every sensory (sightwise) detail can be recalled.

During the advanced sense memory exercises, the actor will learn control of his instrument and become aware of a certain emotional involvement that usually presents itself somewhere in the chain of exercises. This slight emotional involvement is very important. Because of it, we experience different sensations when coming in contact with different objects. An example of this is the sensation felt when coming in contact with an article of great value or an object that is directly involved with our own lives. For instance, we may all objectively understand that an antique vase of the Ming Dynasty was made with the same basic materials provided by nature today and yet, only the most insensitive person would pick up this vase handling it in the same manner as if it were one created by a modern-day craftsman. Consequently, "precious" objects, on stage, invariably have to be made precious to the actor before they can be made to seem precious to the audience. Audiences realize that stage articles are usually made from inexpensive glass or papier-mache and are in actuality worthless.

A deeper study of this will be dealt with in a subsequent chapter on Substitution, but mentioning of it now will suffice to familiarize the reader with the interesting and varied results which can be obtained.

Before any actual study and practice of the exercises in the following chapters are attempted, the actor should complete the work as outlined and suggested in this chapter, either in private or in class. Then, as his work progresses, he should advance to the work in another chapter; any chapter, as there is no set program for learning the Method once Sense Memory is fully understood. I must caution you that a feeling of simplicity should be maintained in all of the exercises in this book.

Every theatrical and acting problem could never be included in one book or in a dozen books. Because of this, I strongly recommend that every actor engage in as much classwork as possible. Again, there is no beginning and no end to learning. This holds true more for the actor than for anyone else. Other professions can be learned from A to Z, but who learns everything about life?

Earlier, I cautioned the actor to consciously avoid any pantomimic gestures while working on the exercises. The reasons for this are many; some are stated before. Pantomime itself is a phase of the theatre that is all too often associated with acting. It should never be. Much to the regret of many serious actors, the term "theatre" is a word that embraces too much. The word seems to encompass any group of people who assemble to observe a show. The word theatre is used to describe ballet, puppetry, lectures, a surgical clinic, mimes, opera, sometimes the circus, and the recitation of noxious verse accompanied by music. Since we are so liberal in our usage of the term "theatre," it is only logical that pantomime performers would fall heir to the term "actors."

In life, our actions are created unconsciously by our inner feeling and emotions. So it must be with acting, with the exception that our feelings and emotions must be dealt with consciously. When this is done, our actions on stage are real and therefore believable. Also, our instruments must be free to express what we feel at the moment and must not be chained to cliche-ridden results.

Pantomime is, by definition, a dumb-show imitation of life. This is clearly not acting. Pantomimic gestures are each carefully plotted out and rendered with redundancy; whereas, actions or gestures on stage should be natural and believable with the same wonderful simplicity of life. The process by which pantomimic actions are created is usually insular and unoriginal and most restrictive to the actor-artist. Because it is supposed to translate the lines in visible symbols, pantomimic results are both trite and banal. Sometimes the audience's attention is diverted by actors who resort to their use, but even then, it does not mean they are truly enjoying it or will remember it in the future.

The actor-artist should be able to draw forth from his reservoir of life's experiences, from his observation of life's natural laws, and from his own emotions to produce reality in the true sense of the word and not be a surrealistic attempt at imitation.

There are many books on acting which advocate the use of pantomime, even going so far as to tell the actor how to move his arms and how to cup his hand in a certain position in order to signal another to approach him. This is incorrect. In life, when calling to someone, we do not stop to plan ahead how to move our hands, arms, neck, and head for our every action. We move them accordingly with the inner impulse that motivates the gesture. Therefore, it is the *motivation* that must be created, which, in turn, regulates the action. There would be nothing artistic, original, or creative in acting if every actor mimed his actions. The reader can see that it would lead to the most commonplace conventionality, making the actor a stereotyped automaton inhibited from any individual freedom of expression or movement.

It is for this individuality that we should strive. The actor can only express his art with his own instrument and with his own sensibilities and awareness. He must never attempt to imitate or copy, but, instead, utilize his own natural actions which invariably are more believable and realistic.

*"How is one to create real passion,
and not its surrogate, not its ugly
theatrical imitation."*
                Stanislavsky

Affective Memory

Actors are a strange lot, a breed apart from their fellow man. For it is only by playing the passions of other "people" and by making them come to life on a stage do they find relief (a temporary one at that) from their gnawing desire to act. They can never go to the theatre with the same desire for mere entertainment as other people. The actor sees more deeply into the play than the average patron around him. He watches, listens, studies, wonders, criticizes to himself, and constantly projects himself into every part he sees. He sees himself as the villain, the hero, the lover; sometimes even playing Iago to his own Othello. It is this innate, insatiable desire to be somebody else for just a few hours a night that usually turns the young person's head toward the theatre. And this reason is a most legitimate one for if it did not exist, neither would the theatre. It is not anomalous that the strength of feeling and desire to act is often tied very closely to the extent to which an actor is able to express his own emotion while on stage.

We come now to that phase of acting which is concerned with the expression of emotion. Being able to express emotion with verisimilitude is for most actors the crux of their analysis and work on a role.

All of us at some time in our careers have had roles that we did not feel comfortable in or did not feel to be close to us as human beings. We felt embarrassed and self-conscious about trying to show anger, love, hatred, joy, or whatever the part called for; and when we would resort to forcing such strong emotions externally, without really feeling or believing them ourselves, it would only seem to make matters worse. We were bewildered as to why a seemingly simple role at first study would turn out to be so difficult and would cause so much anxiety. At other times we can pick up a script and from the first reading feel such an affinity for the lines as to prompt us to remark, "I feel as though the part were written for me alone." All this makes us wonder how and why these differences and indifferences can exist. After all, we are actors and should be able to express the author's wishes with truth and conviction.

The reasons for these imponderables are readily explained with only a faint knowledge of nature's laws. Some people might want to venture that it all hints of a psychoanalytical foundation. This is probably true but at the same time it all boils down (psychoanalysis as well) to the reasoning of nature's laws.

Nature acts as a filter for what is real or unreal to our subconscious in accordance with the past experiences of our own emotions in life. When a line in a play, whether consciously or subconsciously, coincides with something real in our past, we may either express the line with a very truthful reading or be inhibited by it, depending upon its relation to and impact on our personal feelings. It is the awareness of these feelings, the releasing of any inhibitory factors connected with them, and the creation of genuine emotion that will be discussed in this chapter.

The terms *Affective Memory* and *Emotional Memory* are identical in meaning. I choose to use Affective Memory out of deference to my teacher and also out of ease in putting this book together. The existence of Affective Memory as well as Sense Memory has long been perceived, but it is to Konstantin Sergeyevich Stanislavsky that the credit belongs for direct application to acting.

Affective Memory is the conscious creation of remembered emotions which have occurred in the actor's *own* past life and then their application to the character being portrayed on stage. I shall explain this process of creating emotion and how it may be applied by several exercises.

In order to make a character come *alive* on stage, the emotions, thoughts, and feelings of the character must be real to the actor. He must learn to search his own past for emotions that will correspond to his character's life.

So many actors try to hide behind their roles and try to lose their identity in their parts that we wonder why they have chosen their profession. The young actor must learn from the first that he can never lose himself on stage. No matter what type of character, no matter how different the character may be from the actor portraying him, he must always remember that he is *playing himself*. For an actor to lose himself in a role would be for him to lose control. This would approach insanity and all reality and verisimilitude would vanish.

Now the reader may wonder how it is possible for an actor to always play himself on stage, especially since many emotions that are required may not have been experienced by the actor in his own life. Also, many characters will differ so greatly from him. I can best clear this up by advising the actor to, conversely, ask himself how it would be possible for him to play anyone else but himself! He can never literally turn himself into the character and he can certainly never take leave of his own body and soul. The actor has to use *his own* feelings, not somebody else's; he has to use *his* body, not another body. The most and the best that he can do is to train his emotions to respond accordingly with the character's emotions. This is why he and his instrument must be trained as one; to find, coax out, and, finally, to reproduce emotions at will, to heighten or lessen them, and to "shade" them to their proper perspective. The ability to recapture emotions in one's past with expedition is sometimes no easy task and the student should pay close attention to the exercises in this book when he comes to them.

By having a "repertoire" of emotional experiences, the actor can call forth, at the proper time, the desired one needed for the character. The broader his "repertoire," the greater the resources for creativeness and the greater the number of roles he will be able to act. He should be able to laugh real laughter, cry real tears, or generally exhibit any emotion with complete reality. Every emotion that has been utilized in his life can be recreated on stage with all or part of its original depth of feeling. Whereas, in life at the time the emotion was happening it might have been uncontrollable, the actor will discover that with proper training his recaptured emotions will be fully controlled by him.

There are several important aspects of Affective Memory that must be known before beginning work on the exercises in this chapter.

Any emotions of a psychological nature should be avoided if they are still fresh in the mind and sensitive to the individual. These include experiences which might cause real mental anguish such as the death of a loved one. In the case of exceptional experiences, as the one just mentioned, it is always wise to choose one that is at least seven years old. This way the emotion is still there, but all personal feelings which ordinarily might give way to hysteria will be under control. It is a strange coincidence that usually the fresher an emotional experience is in our minds, the more difficult it is to explore it fully. Thus, it would be difficult to use it in its proper perspective.

Experiences from childhood are very powerful because they are not often expressed at the time they happened and are lying dormant in full strength. The human mind seems to retain incidents which happened in extreme youth (often in detail) more readily than things that might have occurred only a month ago. This is probably due to the fact that the brain received its impressions when the mind was not cluttered with the rationalizations and defense mechanisms used to ''protect'' and blot out our true feelings as in later adult life.

The experiences you choose should be unusual enough to have left an imprint on your mind and it is up to each individual to decide on their usage. Some experiences which you would expect to produce the emotion as you remember it will turn out to mean nothing to you. These should be discarded. Others, to which you had attached no unusual importance at first consideration, may turn out to be the expression desired and may produce powerful results. You will have to experiment with several past experiences in order to fill your "repertoire."

During the early stages of the exercise work, the experience should be narrated under proper supervision. This is to guide the student in order to make certain that the exercise is being done correctly and, also, to be able to explain and to clarify any puzzling results which occur. An acting class with a qualified teacher is a must for this.

When an exercise is narrated, it should be recreated *verbally* and the exercise is then called, for the benefit of the class, a *Narrative*. However, when applied to scene work or to an actual role, it is, of course, not narrated and is spoken of as an Affective Memory. Once a Narrative is found to be full of the emotional response desired, it can then be applied directly to a role. The process and accompanying procedures for this will be found in Exercise II of this chapter, but Exercise I should be worked on several times until it is made as full as possible.

I must also caution you not to expect consistent results with the Affective Memory exercise until the instrument has been trained to recreate. There is more to becoming an actor than just having theatrical photographs made and "making the rounds" for work. You have to be able to back up any qualifications that you may present. It sometimes takes as long as two or three years of study to fully train the actor's instrument in all phases of the Method. Of course, a great deal depends on the individual and some actors possess the necessary sensitivity and perception that facilitates their training to a bare minimum of time. It is rare, though.

This is not meant to sound discouraging, but acting is a profession that must be learned with consistent study and training just as any other profession is learned. A doctor thinks nothing of devoting eight to twelve years in study, a lawyer from six to eight. So you see, the actor is rather fortunate from that point of view and, at the same time, the spiritual and artistic demands, not to mention the financial, can be equally rewarding.

Before beginning the exercises, you must realize that no emotion can be created by trying to recapture the emotion directly. It must be taken in steps with complete disregard for the *end results*.

Sometimes during a performance, by pure accident, a genuine feeling of emotion will sprout from out of nowhere. The actor will be exhilarated and feel that he has actually "lived" his part and created it most realistically, which he probably did. These moments of inspiration are wonderful to experience. They show that the actor's imagination was working and that his inner feelings were probably well in tune with the play. But what happens at the next night's performance? He goes out on stage and when his big scene arrives, he tries to remember the same feeling, the same emotion that he experienced the night before. He is usually quite surprised and sometimes embarrassed because none of the spontaneous qualities from the previous night appear. What the actor did wrong was to *anticipate the end result* instead of trying to recapture the circumstances that *led to the end result*.

Accidental inspirations are very refreshing, both to the actor and to the performance, but, unfortunately, they are all too rare and undependable. Therefore, the actor must first learn that emotion cannot be reproduced by thinking of or remembering the emotion itself. Emotion can only be reproduced by concentrated effort to remember *each circumstance* and *each sensory step* that produced the emotion originally.

The following exercise is a Narrative to be done as a part of classwork only. The reader will notice how Sense Memory is utilized in every Affective Memory exercise. This will be true in nearly every phase of the Method.

In the chapter on Sense Memory, I chose specific exercises for you to begin your work. I cannot choose a specific experiment from the actor's past life to begin work on Affective Memory. This must be left to the individual. I can only guide the steps to be taken. Therefore, pick an experience out of your past life; one that is at least seven years old, one that you believe would cause you to cry *real tears* if relived.

EXERCISE I

(A) Sit in a straight-back chair. Assume a comfortable position where you could fall asleep if need be.

(B) Close your eyes and make the same effort to relax, both physically and mentally, as you did in the Sense Memory exercises.

> NOTE: You must again be cautioned not to think of the experience in terms of a story to be narrated. Only the sensory steps are ever narrated. Be concerned only with these sensory sensations and only relate them to the class. For example, do not say, "I feel cold." That is too general. Try to remember exactly where you feel cold, to what degree, what kind of cold it is; a chill or a biting cold? Be as specific as possible. Try to remember exactly what it is that makes you want to say, "I feel cold."

(C) Define the area or areas relating to the experience. For instance, if it took place in a certain room, describe what you saw in the room; if the room was warm, where did it cause you to feel warm? What colors do you see? What odors? What can you hear? What things did you touch or feel? Try to bring all the senses into play.

(D) If the experience took place outside, try to remember the feeling of the sun, air, wind, or rain, against your body. Be aware of the temperature, heat, and cold.

(E) Remember any physical objects you saw during the experience. This could include a person, but never say, "I saw a man." Again, this is too general. Instead, describe by Sense Memory what you, your instrument, saw with your senses.

(F) Remember the voices or sounds you heard during or leading up to the "experience." Do not repeat the words. Only describe your sensory reaction to them: the sense of hearing, the tone, the pitch, etc.

> NOTE: It is again imperative to remind you that as the exercise progresses, you should absolutely not anticipate the end result (in this case, the tears). Keep the concentration trained on all the sensory events that lead to the emotion.

(G) Try to remember anything you touched or that touched you. Describe them fully with the senses. Do not say, "I am touching a desk," without describing its shape, texture, color; be conscious of anything touching you like the feel of your clothes on certain parts of your body, the dust on your fingertips, etc.

(H) If pain or a sense of pain is involved, describe its exact location. If it moves, decreases, or increases, if it is a dull pain or a sharp pain, try to remember the sensations clearly as you narrate them.

(I) After you have recalled every sensory object that you are able to, and the climax of the exercise is reached, terminate it.

You and your teacher will be able to decide if the exercise was wholly successful or not. This will depend upon the strength of the experience to your subconscious emotions and whether or not your concentration was fully working.

Go back over the Affective Memory in your mind and try to recall any "objects" of the five senses you may have omitted. Sometimes you will find it easier to remember other pertinent areas of the experience after the exercise is finished. These should be included the next time the exercise is attempted.

You may also discover a result which is very different from what you expected. As I stated previously, the experience may by this time have no meaning to you, thus having no value to you as an actor. On the other hand, the Affective Memory may have resulted in a type of emotion which is just the opposite of the kind you worked to reproduce. Laughter or extreme happiness would be an example of the above instance. Nature has a strange way of changing things around from the way we sometimes remember them. If such a thing occurs, by no means think the exercise is valueless. On the contrary, it means that you have found an experience for another emotion and this opposite emotion can certainly be utilized for the emotion that was produced.

There may be variations or "shadings" of emotion in the exercise. These should be carefully noted by the teacher and brought to the attention of the student-actor. They, too, can be used for the effect that was achieved.

Each exercise should be repeated until it has become familiar to the mind and its sequences have become logical and orderly. After repeating it several times, you will discover that each time the emotion will be slightly different from the previous time. In life we do not always laugh with the same amount of joy each time we laugh, or laugh exactly the same way each time. Neither do we cry with the same amount of tears each time we experience sorrow. Instead, the intensity of the emotion is regulated by our state of mind at the time the changes take place and by the strength of the experience as it affects us.

Therefore, do not think about the feeling which was achieved in last night's performance. The emotion will always occur if the work is properly done, but any differences or variations should be noted and even expected. The overall feeling that is being worked for will definitely present itself to the audience, but the actor will have to train himself to regulate it. If the actor dwells on the feeling or emotion to be expressed or if he *anticipates* the emotion, the concentration will be lost on the sensory steps that lead *to* the emotion. When the concentration on these steps is lost, the emotion cannot appear.

The subject of training the actor's concentration will be taken up in a later chapter devoted to that alone. Several points concerning the training of the actor's concentration will prove helpful to Affective Memory exercises.

At this point, the reader may be slightly confused as to how Affective Memories are directly applied to an author's words. The actor is on a stage, saying the words in his script, but you are wondering how he can remember, step by step, the sensory aspects of an Affective Memory while at the same time remembering to say the author's words. To clarify this question, I shall say: Yes, this is exactly what must be done. I admit that at first glance this seems to be a prodigious task. But it can be done, and quite easily, after a little practice and training. For the time being, do not concern yourself with this problem for it will be fully explained and simplified in Exercises II and III of this chapter.

Only children have the ability to turn emotion off and on seemingly at will. Give a crying child a toy and the tears will immediately stop as his attention is attracted to the object. If the toy is taken away, the tears will flow immediately once again. Their purely honest approach to life indicates how society inhibits the individual as he grows older, repressing the emotions. The inhibitions must be retrained and eliminated by the actor. Often there is a rather therapeutic after-effect to the Narrative Affective Memory exercises, especially after deeply personal experiences have been recalled and brought to the surface. The results usually leave a "good feeling," a feeling of having rid the soul of some particular unpleasantness. Rarely, if ever, will an exercise leave the actor with a feeling of depression, but it is because of this possibility that a qualified teacher should supervise the exercises in the early work and guide the student toward the correct emotional experience. There will be some emotional areas which are better left untapped if there is any possibility of their causing damage or anxiety to the actor.

Happily enough, there is a dual emotion which the actor-artist will always experience during a successful Affective Memory. For while he is attaining his real tears, possibly sobbing his heart out, inside he will feel pure joy. His actor's sense will tell him of the reality and truth he is creating. The realization that he is now truly *acting* will sustain him in the arduous work and study that lies ahead.

For those who still might not fully comprehend Exercise I in this chapter and its purpose, possibly due to the seemingly intangible qualities involved, the following true story should serve to elucidate how a Narrative should progress and should clear up any questions regarding its functions in acting. Because actors seem to have a great deal of sensitivity and are often troubled by occurrences that require self-awareness to their own problems, the reader will realize the possible therapeutic value of Narratives to the actor.

The young lady named Therese, who I am about to discuss, is not an actress. She is a highly intelligent, sensitive individual who possesses a great love for the theatre and for good acting in particular.

One evening we were talking about the Method and its components when she expressed curiosity about Affective Memory. She wanted to know how it worked and after I explained it as best I could, she wanted to know if it would be possible for her to do an Affective Memory exercise in the form of a Narrative. I assured her that anyone could do the exercise if they knew the proper steps in the past experience that led to the emotion *and* if they carried them out properly. It so happened that I was familiar with her background and when she expressed doubt about being able to choose an experience, I offered to choose one for her.

The experience involved the fact that her mother had been divorced while Therese was still a baby. When she reached the age of six years old, her mother remarried. Her new stepfather was anxious to adopt the little girl. This, of course, would change her name. This meant that the real father, whom she had never seen, would have to give his consent. A subsequent meeting between the parties was arranged in a lawyer's office.

Now, when I first suggested this past experience to Therese, she stated that she could not remember very much of what happened and was afraid that because of this, the exercise would not be successful. I told her not to worry about any results and that they would come if she kept her concentration on the sensory objects.

I instructed her to relax in a chair, close her eyes, and since she did not know how to conduct the exercise herself, to concentrate on my questions and let me guide her.

We began the exercise with her arrival at the building which housed the lawyer's office. Her sensory impressions of this building were vague to the extent that she remembered only the basic design of the facade and a sort of greyish color connected with the portals and doors.

At my request, she described the heat of the sun on her head, where it felt warm on her face, neck, shoulders, and arms. Upon entering the building, the all-encompassing coolness of the air inside seemed to replace the intense heat that prevailed just a moment before with a slight chill. When we "entered" the lawyer's office, her memory worked so well that I could see the wonderment on her face. At first recollection, the strongest sense that she recalled was the smell of the room. The mustiness, the books and furniture, all came back with an almost suffocating fullness.

I then asked her to give descriptions of all the things she could remember seeing in the room. She began with the dark green wallpaper that had a little white design in it, the hundreds of books lined up in wall cabinets with glass doors so they could not be touched. She then remembered the dark green carpeting on the floor, worn in spots, and decidedly a different shade of green from the walls.

Abruptly, amidst these recollections, she remembered she was left alone in this part of the office. I asked her to describe how she felt physically at this moment of privacy. She could only remember a dull ache in her stomach which she now termed as "anxiety."

I returned her thoughts to the carpeting in the room. Out of nowhere she told me how it felt against a bare foot. After twenty years, she had suddenly recalled slipping a shoe off and wiggling her toes on the rug.

Next, I queried her as to any sounds that she could hear. She clearly remembered voices coming through a large brown door that led to another room. She could not remember actual words, but distinctly received the impression of voices soft at first, muffled, then sometimes rising to an angry pitch.

I then asked her to tell me what she was wearing at the time. She told me she was wearing a new blue and white dress, the prettiest dress she had. She then went on in fantastic detail and gave the design of the dress, the pleats, where it was starched, how the sleeves were puffed at the shoulders. She described how it felt across the back, arms, and waist. She gave a full sensory description of the new crisp white petticoat not forgetting to add that she was wearing new yellow panties. She had on white cotton socks and brand new black patent-leather shoes with a little silver buckle. Then she described every sensation involving the wearing of these new clothes down to a slight pinch in her left toe caused by the new shoes.

She remembered how soft her long hair felt on the back of her neck where she had combed it for over an hour.

Obviously, she had dressed with great care for a little child, and had tried to make herself as pretty as she could. I knew there had to be a reason for this and suspected that in her child's mind she had wanted to look pretty for her father, a father she had always wanted but had never known, possibly thinking that if he saw how pretty she was he would come back to *her*.

Therese's Narrative continued with the feeling of sitting in a large leather chair, a description of its sleek coolness against the back of her legs, and a description of the dark brown leather. I then asked her to tell me where she felt warm now and where she felt cool. She described a feeling of warmth at the back of her neck, slightly brushing her hair up as she told me. At the same time she felt cold around her bare legs. Even her feet felt damp in her shoes.

With these last descriptions came an awareness of something she had forgotten about the room. Suddenly, she could hear the ticking of an old wall-clock, one of those short-pendulum clocks with a large white face set in a dark walnut frame that are so often in legal offices.

Therese said then that she felt the same dull ache in her stomach, the "anxiety," the consciousness of just sitting and waiting.

My own anxiety began to grow as I realized that the exercise was almost over. Very quietly I asked her if she was waiting *for someone*. She answered in an almost inaudible whisper, "Yes."

I knew it was now or never. With my next question, I pulled the stopper that released twenty years of pent-up emotion.

I asked, "Who are you waiting for?"

With a gasp choked by tears in her soul as well as her eyes, she answered in the voice of a little girl who had been hurt beyond consolation.

Two words washed with tears tore themselves from her heart. She cried, "My daddy." This was accompanied with the most heart-rending sobs I have ever heard.

The emotion was as equally powerful, vibrant, and full as if the experience had just taken place. Of course, in a sense it did just take place. Her concentration was working very well and she relived the experience in her own mind through her concentration on the sensory objects.

I then spoke to Therese, reminding her that the exercise was finished and congratulated her on what she had done. She had achieved complete reality in an Affective Memory exercise. The second I terminated the exercise, her tears stopped, her face brightened, and it was only several moments before she said that she felt "wonderful." This last remark is what, to some, seems incredible when doing these exercises.

Later, Therese informed me that her father had not appeared at the lawyer's office. Instead, he had sent the necessary papers for the adoption to proceed without him because he chose not to be present. This was, of course, taken by the child to be a rejection of her, but at the time it happened, she had *not* cried, had not shown any outward emotion at the obvious rejection, and had literally "held it inside" for twenty years. Consequently, after finally expressing the emotion in the form of an Affective Memory exercise or Narrative, the emotion was released and because of this she felt "wonderful." This feeling is really quite common when we are able to release our anxieties and pent-up emotions.

I might add that Therese told me several months later that a much better relationship now existed between her and her stepfather. This undoubtedly was due to the new awareness she had of herself.

The actor, too, must constantly strive for this self-awareness. He must learn in life not to keep his feelings and emotions imprisoned but to give vent to expression, even at the risk of violating inane social conventions. Eventually, every natural, honest feeling will transfer itself to the beholder in life, as indeed it will on stage, and give the actor the freedom of his instrument, the individuality as opposed to conventionality that he so desperately requires for a full and creative artistic life. The problem of being able to free the emotions in life and on stage will be taken up in more detail in a later chapter devoted to actor's problems. However, one element needed to achieve this kind of freedom is the preclusion of any situations which might lead to an insular life. He must never isolate himself from the material to be acquired by the varied company of other people for this is the main source of knowledge. All walks of life should be explored for the myriad material they possess. Likewise, he should never be satisfied with acting as the only art on which to focus his interest.

Indeed, the modern actor must develop a gulosity for material which is derived from everything around him. Besides searching his past and its experiences for material, he must benefit from the commonplace as well as the arts. Everything should hold an interest for him. Ballet, opera, concerts, art galleries, museums, newspapers, folk dances, scientific achievements, history, world affairs should be indulged in concurrently, studied and added to the vast store of knowledge needed for the actor's creativity. Needless to say, the actor's work is never really done. It is with these opulent experiences that the actor's instrument can remain youthful, his spirit fresh, his performances adroit.

After you have practiced your Narrative in class several times and are satisfied that it has been properly done, the time comes for you to begin work on transferring it to appropriate dialogue. To reach this phase of Affective Memory work, it is necessary to proceed through a lay-over stage. This lay-over stage will be explained in Exercise II while Exercise III will be the final process used for actual stage work. Both Exercises II and III can be practiced and utilized in scene work for an acting class but are done mentally, not verbally like a Narrative. They can be worked on privately or in re-hearsal.

EXERCISE II

(A) First prepare yourself mentally by completely relaxing and clearing the mind of anything but the Affective Memory you have chosen.

(B) Pick an actual physical task, not a sense memory task, to do throughout the exercise. As an example, girls can apply lipstick, powder, rouge or a whole make-up operation; if at home, you can pick a task such as housecleaning. Boys can pick tasks such as getting dressed, cutting the grass, sweeping a floor, anything you may do in relative privacy that is familiar to you and requires a minimum of concentration.

(C) The actor may now begin either the physical task first or the Affective Memory, whichever is better for him. For the purpose of this exercise, we begin with the physical task.

(D) As the physical task is being done, begin the Affective Memory exercise. Start at the very beginning of the exercise and retrace slowly with the inner concentration all the sensory objects you found in the Narrative that created your emotion.

(E) Follow these steps to the conclusion you desire while keeping the instrument "open" to free expression of the physical task.

> NOTE: If the Affective Memory exercise is one to create unhappiness or tears, as in Exercise I, you will find that the physical task accompanying the exercise will be duly affected. In other words, in life we do not get dressed in exactly the same way when our spirits are high as we do if they're low.

(F) When the emotion appears, do not stop the physical task. Make the effort to keep the task going and let the emotion rule the way the task is done.

(G) Keep this result going for as long as you think necessary for the development of the exercise. Usually five or ten minutes is long enough once the emotion has been established.

Also, become aware of how the inner emotion affects the physical task.

You will notice that the Affective Memory exercise and the physical task combine at the end result to form an etude of purely realistic art. The result will be original and fresh. It will show how *you* put on your lipstick, sweep your floor, or whatever physical task you chose, not how you have copied the task from someone else. This phase of the work is essential in training the actor's originality. He must never try to copy someone else but, instead, strive to represent his own instrument through his own body.

Exercise III will pertain to the direct application of Affective Memory to dialogue. The dialogue chosen should be the actor's choice, but I would advise him to choose it for simplicity at first.

Again, as in Exercise II, have the sensory steps which lead to the emotion as firmly in mind as you have the dialogue which accompanies it. When learning the lines of dialogue, it is important to learn them simply without any prescribed feeling or interpretation.

EXERCISE III

(A) Make the same effort as in Exercise II to relax, both mentally and physically. The exercise may be done either sitting or standing but without doing any physical tasks.

(B) Begin the exercise keeping the inner concentration on all the sensory steps.

(C) Now add a line or two of the chosen dialogue. Do not pay any attention to the way the dialogue is spoken. In other words, do not anticipate the end result or try to show emotion through the words.

(D) If at first you seem to lose the concentration on the Affective Memory exercise, return to it and keep going.

(E) As the exercise progresses, add a few more lines of dialogue.

(F) Now make the effort to retain the past experience at the same time you speak the dialogue. By this I mean try to combine the two and keep both going at the same time. Do not worry if one of the two slips away. If this happens, just relax and return to one, slowly attempting to incorporate both.

(G) After the emotion reaches its climax, speak the rest of the lines *through* the emotion. Do not try to give added punch or impetus to the lines, but let the lines come out of the emotion that you have created, just *the same way it happens in life*.

NOTE: When we cry in life, we usually try to keep from crying. To the beholder this only makes us seem to be crying more. When we cry, but at the same time try to speak in a normal voice, the effect is one of pure sadness whereas if we "cried" only with our voice the impression is one of fake crying. If we try to "cry" with our voices in a wailing, moaning fashion doing the Affective Memory exercise, the impression becomes one of wild hysteria. Therefore, simplicity should be maintained in the exercise.

When the emotion is finished, go back in a short time and repeat it, all the time adding more lines of dialogue and closing any inconsistent gaps and unnecessary pauses.

This exercise should be repeated until the actor can keep his concentration on the exercise and freely speak the author's words at the same time.

Now, the reader may justifiably wonder how it is possible to keep the mind on two things at once: the past experience *and* the author's lines. It is only slightly difficult at first, until the instrument has been trained to do so, but certainly far from impossible. We do it all the time in life. We all, at some time or another, have carried on a conversation with someone while at the same time have had our minds on something else like what we did last night or what we are planning to do tonight. The person to whom we are speaking will get the impression that we are "miles away." This is because the inner emotions, caused by our thoughts on a different subject, do not fit the words that we are speaking.

Have you ever talked to a young girl in the morning after a date with her new boy friend the night before? You may be telling her of a disaster you read about in the newspaper but her reply may startle you, even though the words are of concern, until you realize with amusement that her thoughts are on the previous night's engagement which is infinitely closer to her. The emotion accompanying her words were probably dreaminess and pleasure and not pertinent to the subject you were discussing.

Our inner emotions and feelings are dead giveaways to an untruthful action or spoken word. Therefore, the problem of choosing the correct emotional experience for the stage presents itself. Along with this, there is the problem of fitting the obvious emotion to the situation.

I have repeatedly stressed the necessity of freedom for the actor's instrument and the need for trenchant thought in his observation of life. Now, at the end of this chapter, I must stress an additional quality. This will concern itself with objectivity in any choices to be made. There is a rule of sorts which I believe can aid the actor in much of his future work. This rule is: *In life there is no preconceived right way of doing something; there is no set wrong way; there is just reality!*

Sometimes we decide too quickly the problems of interpreting a role. Sometimes we are wont to choose the easiest solution, usually the obvious one. At other times, we tend to create additional problems when in reality they do not exist. When we do not leave our minds open to reality, we are in danger of giving a conventional stereotyped performance. Let me give two examples of how conventional logic can destroy original creation.

Two diverse roles are presented to the actor. In one of the roles the character has just received very good news. The actor immediately begins to think in terms of happiness, joy, and laughter. In the second role the character has received very distressing news. Consequently, the actor begins to draw up mental pictures of sadness, unhappiness, and perhaps tears that he can produce to ''show'' these emotions.

The question now arises as to whether or not emotional results are to be so clearly drawn in the final analysis of a role. I don't believe this is so for the simple reason that they certainly are not in real life. It is a strange quirk of nature that we do not always laugh when we are happy or necessarily cry when we are sad or unhappy. To illustrate what I mean, let us take the two roles just mentioned and supply them with rather hyperbolic situations.

Suppose that you, the reader, are in a somewhat embarrassing financial predicament. You have just lost your job, have no prospects of another, your savings are depleted, and you know of absolutely no one that you can turn to for even temporary aid, much less a loan. At the very moment when circumstances seem at their bleakest, news reaches you that a rich relative has left you one hundred thousand dollars. When the news of such a sum finally reaches your conscious mind, oddly enough, even though it is very good news, you may not laugh about it. Plausibly, you may just sit down and have a nice quiet prayer or a quiet cry by yourself.

On the other hand, suppose your neighbor runs into your house while you are reading this book and announces in an alarmed voice that your mother had just been killed by a speeding train. Would this bring on a sudden rush of tears? Not necessarily. There might be a stunned expression of disbelief, horror, and finally, when the truth of the announcement is realized, an unconscious, hysterical laughter may emit *without the shedding of a single tear*. This is not to say that tears will not be shed later at the funeral or numerous times in the future when the experience is remembered. In life, when we retell an experience and describe fully all the sensory details of it, the emotion is recreated again in all its intensity. This is the basis of the Affective Memory exercises.

In either of the two extreme cases just cited, the resulting emotion is true and therefore believable. It must be remembered that nature is not conventional, her actions not stereotyped. Nature and her manifestations are original, naturally pure, and beautiful. I also use these two extreme examples to illustrate that if any choice of interpretation has been made and if it is believable by virtue of its *reality* in presentation, then it should certainly be acceptable. I cannot stress enough that original interpretation depends upon the actor's training to create on stage that which is real to him in life. Whenever these problems of interpretive emotions arise, the modern actor must use all the knowledge of life around him to solve them.

Relaxation

Earlier I stated that there is no set pattern for the learning and study of acting which this book might afford. The components which are covered can be studied separately, devoting the necessary time and understanding to each part or combining all the work. It will depend wholly upon each individual's understanding, needs, and limitations. It will also depend upon whether or not he is attending drama classes, on his teacher's way of teaching, and on the individual's relationship to the theatre; if he is a professional or an amateur engaged in community theatre work. Actually, there should be no reason why an amateur should not be able to give as credible and therefore as creditable a performance as a professional actor. This book is by no means limited to just what are commonly spoken of as "professionals."

If you are troubled by the problem of tension, then the contents of this chapter should be thoroughly understood and your own tension problems solved before attempting the exercises in previous chapters or the ones that follow.

The problems of tension beset nearly all actors in life (as it often does almost everyone in life) as well as on stage. Seventy-five percent of being able to accomplish desired stage results depends on relaxation. The actor's natural enemy is tension. It interferes with his inner life, inner feelings, his five senses, and it has a destructive influence on his emotions and creativity.

The two types of tension, physical and mental, are so

closely related and intertwined with each other that at times they are indistinguishable. Mental anxiety can cause physical contraction in the body, and, conversely, the relief of one can bring about the relief of the other. Also, if a single muscle is causing undue pressure, it can throw the whole muscular system off kilter. A stiff neck can creep down to the shoulders, back, and arms. An example of this is doctors who specialize in muscular disorders sometimes relieving pain in certain areas by careful manipulation and ministration to another area which at first does not seem to be connected with the pain. The doctor may make a vertebra adjustment, gently massage the area, or apply heat to it, and as a result, the pain in a shoulder, arm, or neck will disappear.

It becomes necessary to prepare physically so muscles do not obstruct the actor's work. It is impossible to rid the body of all tenseness, and thankfully so. The body would resemble a jellyfish if all tension were gone, but the removal of unnecessary tension should be relentlessly struggled with. This excess tension can and must be controlled by the actor. Awareness of any superfluous tension in his instrument should attract the actor's immediate attention. This awareness of physical contraction must be trained until it becomes second nature, a natural habit which incessantly strives for the removal of tension.

Physical tension cannot be relieved unless you are

(1) Mentally aware that it exists in the first place, and
(2) Aware of its location.

Ordinary muscular spasms and contractions can disappear by gentle massage, stretching, or flexing of the area.

But what about areas such as the throat? Obviously, mental awareness and mental relaxation are needed. Speaking of throat tension, it is not hard to realize the disastrous effect it has on the actor's speech or the singer's voice. A good healthy yawn can release tension in the throat as well as the vital muscles around the mouth that form the actor's words. It can also supply the diaphragm with the exercise it might need.

Tension in the diaphragm can interfere with the actor's breathing and cause shortness of breath.

A classic example of tension interfering with the actor's mental capabilities is illustrated by a task employed frequently by Stanislavsky; but it was Lee Strasberg who personally demonstrated it to me. I had only been studying with him for several weeks when the subject of relaxation was being discussed in earnestness by the class. Doubt as to the seriousness of tension was probably on my face when he asked me to mount the little stage in our classroom.

At extreme stage-right there was an old upright piano. Strasberg then instructed me to go to the piano and lift a corner of it from the floor and to hold it up. As I did so, he gave me a simple mental arithmetic problem involving the multiplication of 65 by 7. My back was rigid, my legs bent, my shoulders and arms full of tension from the physical strain of trying to keep the corner of the piano off the floor. For the life of me I could not keep my mind on the problem, much less give him the answer. He then asked me to sing a song which I had sung in class the day before. I got no further than the first verse. He asked me to recite some poetry. I could not even remember a poem to recite even though he knew I had commited many poems to memory. Needless to say, I needed no further convincing.

The reader can demonstrate this to himself by lifting any reasonably heavy object. Then try to recall all the things you did and saw the day before or just try to remember in your mind's eye all the houses and buildings on your own block.

Another exercise Strasberg demonstrated to the beginner's class was the selection of several actors to walk around the stage. That was all he asked. The first one, a pretty young girl, new to New York and to the theatre, was asked to go up on stage and just walk around. As she did this, she kept wringing her hands and looking back over the footlights expectantly at Lee and the rest of the class. She was the epitome of self-consciousness. She did not know if she should walk fast or slow. Consequently, her walk was ungainly and artificial.

Next he selected another new student, a young man experienced in modeling who had a great amount of self-assurance and assertiveness about him, certainly more than the lovely thing who preceded him. We watched him walk around and around the stage with his brisk air. But every once in a while he would glance out over the lights and then quickly look away. He was obviously doing his best to convince us that he was not self-conscious. When this was called to his attention by Lee, and our laughter, he readily admitted his self-consciousness.

Strasberg then gave both the students a few simple mental tasks to perform while they continued their walking. He asked the girl to think of all the plays she wanted to see that were currently playing. He asked the young man to think of each play he had seen during the past year, who the performers were, and who directed them. They began their little walk again. Every minute or so Lee would check their thinking by asking them pertinent questions, thus making sure they were actually thinking about the tasks he set for them.

What we the class saw was a complete change in their walks. They both began to move naturally and easily. Their faces relaxed, their bodies moved in accordance with their thoughts. They lost all embarrassment due to the task of having something else to think about. The class knew they were watching them as they really were, as they really walked in life. They had lost the need to *act*, but in doing so had begun true behavior, had become alive and very human; this in an unnatural setting, a stage instead of a street. In so doing, they had really begun acting.

This last example illustrated quite graphically to the class that simple mental tasks can produce physical relaxation. Always remember that for an actor to give the appearance of reality, he cannot pretend or make believe he is thinking on stage. His thoughts must be real thoughts in order to produce true and believable actions. Remember too, the audience never knows the thoughts which go on in the actor's mind and any which produce real behavior can and should be utilized.

What happens when the actor does not think real thoughts and allows himself, through tension, to restrict his artistic imagination? Suppose something unforeseen occurs on stage as it invariably will. An actor makes his entrance and accidentally knocks over a vase, breaking it all over the stage. His first reaction is one of horror and panic. But then he realizes that the broken vase has no relation to the scene he is playing and should be ignored. Inwardly, his panic has only heightened to the extent that he will not allow himself to accept the reality of what has happened. He keeps right on with the scene, blithely trying to ignore the broken pieces as if nothing happened. His discomfiture is immediately obvious to the audience and all vestiges of reality vanish. Any emotions that he has been working for will be lost due to tension which arises from the unnatural state in which he now finds himself involved. How much better it would have been for the scene if he had *used* the embarrassment he felt at the time of the accident. After all, in life do we not get embarrassed if we break something in someone else's house? He could have added a few natural words of improvisation, apologizing for his clumsiness, and continued with the author's lines as he calmly picked up the broken pieces. What the audience would then have seen was a real person in a real situation showing real emotion (in this case, his embarrassment). They would probably have left the theatre commenting on the reality of the scene and thinking that the broken vase was a part of the stage "business."

I once saw an amusing situation in a Broadway play which was similar to the one just mentioned. It was even amusing for the actor who is known among friends for his inventiveness as well as his improvisational ability.

In a certain scene he was supposed to remove his coat and casually toss it a few feet over the back of a chair. On this particular night he tossed the coat a little too hard. It missed the chair altogether and it landed in the orchestra pit. There was a discreet silence among the audience until Tony Franciosa was heard to remark, "Well, that's the end of the coat." The spontaneity of the remark convulsed the audience to such a point that the producers and director decided to leave in the whole business for the run of the show.

The effort to relax should not be limited to stage work alone. All through the day you should try to recognize your tensions and eliminate them. Because personal life and the actor's instrument are so closely connected, you can well understand the need for this. An actor who has tension in his legs will enter the stage with a stiff, artificial, "stagey" walk. An inflexible spine will affect the whole back and possibly the shoulders and arms with its rigidity. Tension can even settle in the hands and fingers causing them to become clumsy and to shake. This latter affliction is not to be confused with the nervousness commonly called stage fright. However, stage fright can cause a great deal of tension and nervousness which some actors like to believe gives a sharp edge to their performances. As a whole, it is a very unpleasant occurrence that should limit appearances to special occasions such as opening nights. If an actor prepares himself properly as regards relaxation and concentration on his role, this evil manifestation of idleness will not appear.

When arriving at the theatre, an actor should take enough time in his dressing room to prepare himself for his night's work. Any exercises that are necessary, either mental or physical, to bring about relaxation should be employed. He should pay particular attention to the facial area. The muscles around the eyes should be relaxed. The bridge of the nose, temples, jaws, mouth, and forehead should all be properly relaxed even before applying makeup. Even the tongue can be limbered up by doing a series of stretching exercises. These muscles in and around the face are very important to relaxation. They must be flexible and pliant for the actor's inner life of the character to be able to flow through them with ease of expression. Next, his body must be relaxed in order to avoid the pitfalls already mentioned caused by undue tension in the limbs and torso.

To test your own body for tension, try the following test: Lie flat on the floor on your back. Feel where the pressure is exerted. What parts of the body are actually touching the floor? Most probably only the shoulder blades, rump, and the calves of the legs. This little test can be further demonstrated the next time you go the beach. Lie in some wet sand and then rise very carefully. You will very likely get only a partial imprint of your whole back area. The other parts of your back that do not touch the floor or leave an imprint in the sand are in a state of tension. The spine, back ribs, shoulders, neck, and backs of the knees should all be resting easily against the floor. These areas should be consciously worked on in everyday life, as well as just before going on stage. There are many ways to rid yourself of these tensions but usually a conscious awareness of them will cause the individual to find his own way.

One method used is to start from the toes and go all the way up to the neck, gradually tightening each muscle in the legs and trunk, until you are in a complete state of rigidity. Then, relax every muscle at once. It sometimes helps to do this two or three times in order to get the benefit of complete relaxation.

I remember my father used to say that only two sorts of people could roll down a flight of stairs without a resultant injury; a small baby and a man who is dead drunk. Obviously, the reason for this being the muscular relaxation afforded by the innocence of one and the not-so-innocent condition of the other. Babies and even young children possess the ability to relax at will until, unfortunately, the rigors and mendacious qualities of modern society transform them into a permanent state of tenseness.

Observe what happens if a baby is placed on a pillow or similar soft substance. When picked up, a full imprint of its body will be left as mute evidence of his relaxed state.

Most animals, too, have the innate ability to relax at all times, which is something our nervous society has to learn mechanically. Try the pillow test again, only this time use a cat. Place him on it to sleep or to rest. Carefully raise him and observe the clear outline and imprint of his body. If a human being could relax like this, he could probably get by with only half the sleep he is accustomed to getting.

A cat is one of the most interesting subjects of observation for an actor even if he is not inclined to like cats as pets. Where the human being tends to use all of his muscles in a physical task, the cat will leave every part of his body that is not in actual use, relaxed. He uses only the muscles that are necessary leaving the rest supple and free from strain. When a cat walks, there is no unnecessary or sloppy movement. When he sits back on his haunches and paws playfully at a piece of string, his back shoulders, haunches, and hind legs are relaxed and yet perfectly balanced. Only the paw that is moving is in action and the other paw, until ready to strike, will flex, relax, flex and then relax always with a great conservation of energy. It is this lack of superfluous movement and perfect distribution of energy that accounts for his clear, sharp speed and accuracy when he pounces or springs. I would suggest that the neophyte to acting spend at least several hours in studying the actions, movements, and attitudes of the common house-cat. All animals should be carefully observed and studied as they can lend amazing insight to the actor on problems of relaxation and, strangely enough, on human behavior. Trips to places where animals are in their natural habitats or even to zoos can be most helpful.

The problem of posture is one that whole chapters could be written about, but it is hoped that I have stressed the evils of muscular tension enough that the reader will be made aware that tenseness is a prime contributor to bad posture. Incidentally, bad posture does not necessarily conform to the mental picture of a slouching, bent-over type of person. The person with a rigid spine and celestial tilt to his head can be equally guilty of bad posture if his erectness is not natural to him.

The last phase of relaxation is of paramount importance and significance to the previous chapter on Affective Memory. It might even be termed the "logic of illogic," but it holds true in every case. The effort to relax should be applied with equal determination to the more tense, excitable, and emotional roles as it is to the more docile ones. The average actor believes he can and should work himself up into a frenzy in a certain role in order to display the particular emotion of excitement or a frenzied state of mind. This is hardly true. At the point where he is supposed to be in a frenzy, he must inwardly be in a *relaxed* state to allow the objects of his concentration to flow through his instrument and give the impression of being heated or frenzied. This is very important to remember. Many actors make the mistake of preparing emotions for a scene and then forgetting the elements of relaxation which will allow the emotion to appear.

Tension is a mental crippler and can block out all the preparatory work the actor has done. The reader can imagine how impossible it would be to supply all the subtle emotions, all the delicate nuances which are required by a difficult and complicated role if an actor has not correctly relaxed his mind and body.

Concentration

Just as the two kinds of relaxation, physical and mental, are so closely related, so it is with concentration and relaxation as a whole. The actor will find that one cannot exist without the aid of the other. An actor needs relaxation to achieve stage concentration and he must certainly concentrate on either mental or physical exercises to promote relaxation.

Concentration by definition is the act of centering one's attention on an object in order to condense it into a smaller but stronger quantity. For stage work, however, this "stronger quantity" can be made to appear not only "condensed" but expansive as well.

In our work on concentration, we shall start with the first problem that invariably attacks the young actor, that of the yawning proscenium arch. The open space of the proscenium arch is a distraction that has been known to plague actors intermittently throughout their careers. Therefore, before actual stage work is to be done, it is necessary to obliterate the audience by creating mentally an additional wall to the stage setting. This Fourth Wall, as I call it, can be "built" by the use of *Sense Memory*. Again and again in this book you will see how nearly every facet of the modern Method depends upon Sense Memory as its substructure.

In the case of an indoor setting, all the actor has to do to create the Fourth Wall is to set himself simple sensory tasks in "seeing."

Pick a familiar wall from your own room at home and

replace it mentally on stage. As you look toward the audience, try to see the color of the wall, the pictures hanging on it, the borders and boundaries of any objects in that direction, or whatever else is necessary to create if for you. The result of this will be twofold. Not only will it seal your consciousness from the audience, but it will also lend the authentic air that what the audience is seeing is happening behind the privacy of a four-walled room and not just on an open stage.

When an actor is really "seeing" on stage, the audience instinctively knows it, believes what he is doing, and follows his gaze and concomitant thoughts. Concentrating on these simple tasks and following them through by just making the basic effort to see them can start a performance off in just the right direction. At times this concentration may lag and, in order to escape the audience, the actor must return to the basic principles of relaxing, then returning his attention to the stage and the tasks at hand (in this case, his concentration).

Nearly every action on stage is subject to strain due to the knowledge and awareness of the audience's presence. Because of the strain, we find it difficult to establish concentration on such simple tasks as seeing certain real objects on stage. If you are not careful, the items that you are supposed to see will be skipped over. The actor must learn how to look at objects and how to apply his concentration in seeing.

A good exercise for a student to use in training his concentration is having his teacher choose an object for study and observation. The student will have a certain length of time (say, thirty seconds) to observe an ordinary object such as a lamp, a painting, a chair, or a table and then, without looking at the object, give a description of its colors, lines, or general form, any characteristics and as much in detail as possible.

The student will probably be very surprised at the amount of detail and characteristics he failed to notice on the first few attempts at this exercise. After he becomes aware of the colors in a chair, the lines and general form of it, the kind of wood, the texture, the materials used to manufacture it, and even the history relating to its style, the actor is then ready to have the length of time he used to gather these observations shortened. Different objects will be utilized until a strange one can be given and his observation is acute to the point of four or five seconds for a full description of the object. This, of course, requires consistent training on the actor's part, but since work that employs the attention of an object aids concentration it is an integral part of our work. As this work advances, the actor will find that he can expand his concentration by the use of his imagination so that he can bring the objects into a more personal perspective. When I previously mentioned the history surrounding the styling of a chair in the actor's observation of it, I was not being facetious. Have we not all at sometime or another seen an object of interest that made us stop and examine it more penetratingly than as to just its surface characteristics? An ornate spindly gilt chair from the Court of Louis XV will arouse all the mental pictures of the material splendor during those bygone days to one person's imagination while a simple lava-pocked amulet worn by a Pompeian slave will evoke a chain of imaginary situations to someone else.

Let me tell you about a time when I was walking down West Fourteenth Street in New York City. It was late on a summer night and the street was nearly empty. From the other side of the street I heard the sound of laughter; that wonderful joyous kind of laughter that seems unable to contain itself any longer. I looked up and saw, across the street, high up in a tenement building, through an open window, a woman illuminated by a light bulb that was hanging from the ceiling. She was tossing a baby in the air at arm's length, catching and kissing it almost simultaneously. Both were laughing and gurgling, obviously enraptured with each other. I stood transfixed at this scene. I knew that the neighborhood was predominantly Latin American and quite poor and because, subconsciously, I wanted it to, my imagination projected a scene to my mind's eye of the Nativity.

Babies are usually fast asleep at such a late hour (it was past midnight). What I saw was a Spanish woman so filled with love for her baby son that she literally could not wait until morning to play with him! The shabbiness and obvious poverty of the neighborhood disappeared and in its place an opulency of love seemed to prevail through this modern-day madonna and child.

As I recall this scene now, I realize that everything my imagination assumed at the time could very possibly be wrong. If the woman was not even the mother of the child, the whole imaginary situation I had developed would be false and in its place an entirely different reality developed. But this is not the point. I wanted to let my imagination take over and see things in a purely theatrical light that would be more interesting to me than any other and of a quality more suited to my work in the theatre. The actor has artistic license to find material which stimulates his emotions and to keep this material until needed. The imaginary life I gave to my object of concentration proved stimulating to the concentration itself because of the emotional overtones my imagination furnished.

An actor's concentration has to be developed with regard to everyday life in order for it to work fully on the stage. He must see deeper into life's complexities than the ordinary person and this observation and its results are what help to build a strong concentration. When an object of interest attracts him, he must rise above the average person in life and learn to focus his attention so that his powers of observation will be improved. He must not be afraid to examine and question an object. For out of perspicacious observations comes the insight and wealth of material so sorely needed for the actor's mental storehouse.

In the previous chapter I mentioned only slightly the problem of stage fright. Stage fright is a direct result of lack of concentration. As soon as an actor's concentration is directed on the work, all nervousness such as shaky hands and "butterflies" in the stomach will disappear. The next time you feel nervous in a situation, pick an object, a physical object like a fifty-cent piece and begin examining it minutely for its physical characteristics. Take in its size, shape, weight, design, all the grooves and scratches, and basic ingredients. Ask yourself questions regarding the above physical characteristics and then apply your concentration to answering them. Do this thoroughly, keeping the concentration solely on the object. You will soon become aware that the nervousness has left you simply because the concentration was directed to something else beside the situation which caused the nervousness.

Now, in the case of stage fright, do not think that I mean you should try, much less be able, to forget the reality of the audience's presence. For me to say this would be analogous to a mental game played in childhood whereby you were told not to think of the word ''elephant'' for just a single minute. The result was, of course, that no one could keep from thinking of the word elephant since it was the whole mental focal point and purpose of the game. This is not the case here. No, an actor can never forget the audience. But I do stress the fact that while he is aware of his duties for the evening's performance, he must also be able to coalesce this reality with his concentration in order to sustain the tasks he has so diligently prepared. This can be done quite effectively by the aforementioned exercise or one of your own choosing that you have found to be effective. Each actor can, if led in the right direction, find his own concentration and relaxation exercises which are best suited to his own needs, exercises that have a calming and yet focal-centering influence on his instrument.

In the elaborately well-equipped studios of the Moscow Art Theatre of the 1930's, there were technical facilities available for the young actor's training that would seem far advanced to the Western theatre today. The training thirty years ago of the Russian actor was, of course, directed by the State as it is today. However, due to Stanislavsky's writings, more is known of their theatre then than is known generally of their present day techniques. Under the direct tutelage and supervision of Stanislavsky, actors were trained over a longer period of time than is adjudged practical in the Western theatre. It is a known fact that the top echelon of actors in Russia trained over extremely long periods of time, to our way of thinking, to create classic and even popular characterizations. Sometimes an actor would train and rehearse a role for as long as two years before ever stepping in front of an audience! Technical training such as this, with elaborate and complex mechanical facilities, was probably well suited to Russian actors and to some of their productions whose ''runs'' almost approached being endurance contests.

Stanislavsky describes, in *An Actor Prepares*, one of the many mechanical inventions used by the young students in the Moscow Art Theatre. This was a contrivance for training the concentration. It was a Circle of Lights and the area bordered by the circle was sometimes spoken of as the Circle of Attention.

The Circle of Lights is a series of spotlights strategically placed on the stage of the classroom. When the actor sits on the darkened stage, he is engulfed in a circle of light which arcs just in his immediate area. If he is sitting at a table, just the table and his chair are in the circle, leaving the rest of the stage in total darkness. The reason for this was to train his attention to affix itself to his immediate tasks and objects of concentration. As he rises and moves about the stage, always keeping his concentration on the tasks that were given him, the swinging lights follow, helping to keep his attention inside the lighted area only. Since he could barely distinguish objects outside the Circle of Lights, this was purported to give him a greater sense of concentrated feeling. And as his concentration improved and developed, the arc of light was widened until it eventually covered the whole stage.

This sort of mechanical training is probably all well and good and would tend to build a great deal of confidence in the actor's ego, but at the same time it is not hard to see how such prolonged training would be most impractical for the Western theatre whose productions are often considered complete after only four or five weeks of rehearsals.

Therefore, in some cases of the training set forth by Stanislavsky, an abbreviated method had to be found to suit our needs. The results obtained from these abbreviated forms were found to be most suitable and equally effective as compared with the original complex exercises employed by the Russians. Whereas we eliminate much of Stanislavsky's basic work as being impractical, we make up for it by stressing other phases of his system that will produce the same quality of results, only in a shorter interim. Such is the case with his Circle of Lights.

We have found that if the precepts of Sense Memory are learned and strengthened even more so than Stanislavsky emphasized it, mechanical contrivances such as spotlights are unnecessary in developing the concentration. In the first place, these devices eventually have to be abandoned during an actual performance, but if we directly apply Sense Memory to the actor's initial training he can learn to create a Sensory Circle which can remain and be utilized even during a performance.

In order to create your Sensory Circle, you must combine Sense Memory with concentration and draw an invisible line around yourself. Then use your imagination to mark the boundaries you set for your circle and make the effort to keep the concentration inside its borders. As for progress, the circle can be enlarged to enclose more objects, eventually encompassing all or, as you wish, just a part of the stage.

Sometimes the circle you set must encompass more than the stage itself. The Sensory Circle then has a distinct advantage over the old Circle of Lights. But you ask how this is possible. Suppose the scene played on stage is that of the characters being stranded in a lifeboat or on a desert isle with thousands of miles of sea around them. The senses must not be limited to just the strip of land or even limited to just the sea around them. The senses of seeing, for instance, would be expanded to a circle that would border an imaginary horizon on all sides. But, in between this imaginary horizon would be waves, clouds, wind, and birds, all waiting to be created by the actor. Then, too, the sense of sound and even smell would be employed for these senses can detect pending changes in the weather or the approach of a ship which our sense of sight might overlook.

As for the distant horizon, Sense Memory must then be employed to recall the sense of seeing at a great distance. To test this, pick any object from memory that you remember seeing from far away and keep the inner concentration on the object. Then, try to place it before your eyes, seeing it in detail. Ask yourself pertinent questions as to its details, characteristics, and even general description. You will become aware of your eyes feeling exactly the same way they do when looking far away. They would not feel this way if a change were not taking place. Actually, they will be focusing differently than if they were seeing something up close. Your eyes will be almost in the same state as if they were really seeing something at a great distance after the first attempt at the exercise. After only a little practice, you can develop this procedure to the point of duplicating the eye dilations to the pupil that are peculiar to the individual. I once saw an actress create distant sights over the footlights that were so convincing that I was literally compelled at one point to look over my shoulder.

If, in the problem of the expansive circle, that is, one reaching beyond the stage itself, your concentration fails at the border, immediately *make the effort* to find it, perhaps by bringing the object in closer. The danger of losing the concentration in this instance is that it will cause a blankness in the eyes which will give you away and perhaps break the mood you have created for the audience.

For the majority of actors, the Sensory Circle is seldom needed for stage work except sometimes during rehearsals or for roles that contain the problems just discussed. However, I have found it to be the mainstay not only for myself but for many television actors. The need is great for a "protective" little circle that can blot out the many distractions in this medium of acting. And, incidentally, this holds true for actual performances on television as well as rehearsals. The problems involved in concentration during a television rehearsal are, at best, disconcerting. In order to sustain a characterization, you must contend with the constant adjusting of lights, the limitless strands of spaghetti-like cords strewn over the floor that always seem to be trying to trip you, noisy cameramen endlessly adjusting their instruments in your face, technicians of every description scurrying about you, and of course, the limited amount of time allowed for the show's over-all production. The average one hour dramatic television program has no more than ten days rehearsal and usually gets by with just one week. As rehearsals progress, the problems usually manage to get worse instead of better until somehow everything eventually settles down at "air time" and the show goes on. I believe that after any television production is completed, everyone connected with it is secretly just a little amazed that it ever came off at all.

The Sensory Circle is a practical device. The actor carries it with him at all times and, when technical difficulties arise, he can call upon it at will. As his concentration improves, this circle can either be dropped or can be made an integral part of his technique.

The importance that relaxation and concentration play in every phase of acting, from the initial character analysis of a role to the last truthful performance of an extended run, should now be evident. The suggested exercises, to promote relaxation and strengthen concentration in the last two chapters, should be made a part of every actor's work and training.

On Actors' Problems

Actor's roles include certain obstacles and problems which must be solved. These will vary from role to role and these myriad obstacles and problems that confront actors are so diverse that they involve not only immediate acting difficulties but obstacles derived from purely personal and private impediments. Many of these are never recognized by the actor and he will go through life and his career unnecessarily burdened by them. Others are stymied by them and may eventually be defeated by them. Still others will discover their problems and strive to correct them. The actor must learn early in his career that his acting talent (and by this I mean his sensitivity, intelligence, awareness, even his physical attractiveness) will be closely governed by his personal life. Consequently, his personal problems will affect his talents. If these problems are great enough, it stands to reason that they can even affect the course that his career will take. Which course his problems lead him is left to the individual.

Many actors resort to the psychiatrist's couch for the understanding and exculpation of their personal problems. Others may not be fortunate enough to be able to afford this luxury and are forced to resolve them themselves. These "unfortunates," however, who learn to deal with their problems directly, are usually better off in the end because an actor who gains a knowledge of Freudian psychology is not any better off if he still does not recognize the close relationship between his personal life and his acting problems. The truest state of mind becomes false when rested in and the analysand must avoid this end by applying what he has learned to himself.

The condition that governs successful analysis is the same as that which should govern the actor: *facing and emphasizing reality*. This condition receives its verification from nature and her laws. Without trying to sound like an expert on Freudian psychology, which I am not, I do know that the actor who is attracted to a method of acting which relies on nature's laws for the training and development of his instrument usually possesses a mettle wholesome and free from aberrations. I shall not dwell on giving advice on the solution of psychological problems beyond a certain point. Problems such as these are for the classroom, or the analyst, because of their nature. No book should attempt to be applicable to the solution of problems such as these. The actor himself must be aware of any psychological factors present in his acting and learn to deal with them face to face.

In the previous chapters, I have tried to cover several pertinent problems such as the actor's fear of the proscenium arch, stage fright, and problems imposed by the process of familiarizing the reader with the Method. Included in the latter were relaxation and concentration which are big enough problems in their own right.

This chapter will cover many problems that arise during first readings, rehearsals, performances, problems encountered in everyday life, problems in voice, movement, and some rather interesting problems suffered by other actors. Also, several exercises are presented to be used in study and in class work. These exercises can be termed psychological only by virtue of the reflective qualities they afford the actor. Because of these "qualities," which are revealed to the receptive actor, there is very often a common fault that develops among Method actors, a fault which strangely enough is usually absent in actors who rely on other schools of thought regarding acting. This fault is a pronounced tendency to over *intellectualize*. Perhaps this is not so strange after all since the very nature of our work is to delve deeper into a role than is usually done by actors not accustomed to our way of work. Nevertheless, if it is overdone, it is a fault. It is time-consuming and, all too often, leads toward the work being done only in the mind and not allowing it to be expressed throughout the whole instrument. Whereas the conventional actor will not bother at times to use his intelligence in a constructive way, the Method actor will sometimes tend to go overboard. This is because of the importance attributed to a deeper-than-surface study of a characterization.

However, he will soon discover that too much intellectualizing can hinder him from accomplishing any of the tasks he may have set for the creation of his character. This is usually brought about by trying to grasp at one time all the facets of the character he is portraying. When he overburdens himself with too many facets of a character, his own instrument will become blocked and the necessary flow of natural emotion is diverted or even lost. It would be much better for him to pick as little as one or two basic tasks that truly represent his character, and to carry them out with reality, then to load himself down with metaphysics which abound in elaborate subtleties of thought and expression. This problem particularly manifests itself when an actor is portraying a character of seemingly complex proportion. What he fails to realize is that a person's complexities usually stem from only one or two main sources. If these can be fully realized, then everything his character does will be motivated by them. Also, on stage as well as in life, some things must be left to our imagination if a character is to remain interesting and attractive to us. We rarely get to know all the intricacies of another person in life. If we do, all of the enchantment soon takes leave and we find ourselves filled with ennui. The subject of creating a character will be taken up fully in the two chapters devoted to that and is too involved to discuss at length now. I will say that as the actor progresses in his role, he can gradually add other dimensions and tasks to his characterization that will aid his artistic development and also serve to keep his role alive and fresh to the audience.

It is a tragedy of the theatre that after centuries of drama being performed a turgid style of acting still exists. As a whole, we have just not yet learned to paint our real lives on the canvas of the stage. Of course, progress has been made, mostly in the last thirty-five years. Being aware that something is amiss is the first step in overcoming an obstacle.

With the advent of the Moscow Art Theatre under the direct supervision of Konstantin Stanislavsky, this new method of acting spread throughout the world. Much of it has remained the same as when he personally taught it. Some of it has been abandoned, modified, or expanded to meet the needs of a changing society. But, basically, his system has survived intact nearly every abuse that could be found to heap upon it. Even his emphasis on reality, beauty of nature, and the dignity of life have been attacked as being vulgarities simply because his truth was brought to the stage. There have been learned university drama professors who have ignored his teachings; drama coaches, teachers, and others who have twisted and warped his meanings to suit their own selfish individual needs. Actors, too, have rejected Stanislavsky by repeatedly adhering to an exaggerated form of acting. But truth is a terrible adversary for nature is on its side.

Many actors will deny their performances are exaggerated because they have tried to avoid it, but what they do not realize is that the endeavor to be effective or to please easily leads to erroneous behavior on stage. This is but another example of the need for self-awareness.

With this awareness, the realization that exaggeration and turgidity are errors because they are untruths will come.

Because we learn from experience (and through the process of elimination) the next problem we face is just the opposite on a visual level from exaggerated acting, but is actually a form of exaggeration: That of falling below, for underplaying reality.

This, too, is a fault that many Method actors find themselves falling prey to during the course of their training. It has become such a cardinal sin among devotees of the Method to exaggerate anything on stage that many times we are tempted to "play it safe" (to be content with just being natural) rather than to give vent to our expressions even though they would be fully in keeping with the reality of the situation. This is as wrong as overdoing.

However, the logical conclusion would be that a line read naturally and with simplicity is more in keeping with reality than the risk of pushing for a higher degree of emotion which could be phony (until the actor is able to do so with reality). The merits of truth should be our goal; nothing more, nothing less.

The form of exaggeration just discussed is called *Indicating*. A term in more popular use is "over-acting," but this term in itself is contradictory by virtue of the definition of acting to the modern actor. Acting is achieving reality on stage and to overdo this would be to negate it. Indicating includes the application of conventional gestures, conventional vocal expression, or any exaggeration of either one of the two. If the inner life of the character is absent, the actor will find himself resorting to these cliches. The problem of indicating is a serious one for if he is not aware of it, the actor can easily delude himself into believing that he is really "living" the part of his character.

When an actor has prepared his role correctly by solving the problems associated with his character, he is that character while he is on stage. Of course, he should be no less himself at the same time, but not necessarily himself as he is known to the public or even to his friends. He can present his characterization only in proportion to the limitations of his instrument which enables him to give expression to what he feels. His whole success in the full achievement of his characterization lies in his reliance on the reality of his own individual, personal expression as opposed to cliche forms of expression. The actor who relies on nature's endowments and on his own individuality is the creative artist. One who is not trained to individual expression and is unable to use himself to be the character he is portraying but, instead, tries to *act* the part, is usually bound and limited to conventionality in his every expression. His voice will resort to pitches and modulations seldom, if ever, heard in life. He will shake his fists, slap his forehead, cast his eyes spuriously, clench his teeth, grimace, bluster, place his hand over his heart, and declaim emptily. To be emulous of this conventional style of acting which has, unfortunately, become almost a tradition is stultifying. Admittedly, there are actors who frequently indicate with consummate skill. However, these same actors are always the ones who will exclaim that the finest moments of pure creation and artistic enjoyment in the theatre were derived from one of the rare times they felt ''inspired'' in their role and seemed to ''live'' the part.

How much more rewarding it would be to their creative spirit as an artist if they could train their instruments to create *regularly* these impulses!

The most beneficial end an actor can receive from a rarely inspired performance is the knowledge that when the moments of true inspiration occurred in the play, all his other performances were probably falsely portrayed at these points! It is my firm belief that nature is an insurmountable force that cannot forever be repressed but will, instead, sporadically burst forth and give free rein to truth in spite of our illiberalities. Also, it is to some great measure an indication of our society that we do not follow natural laws automatically but, instead, attempt and usually succeed in restraining or changing them. The actor who is desirous of achieving true artistry in his profession should literally strive a lifetime for the truth of his convictions offstage as well as on. He must never be satisfied until he is able to bring to the stage what every human being produces naturally in life.

As much as I have stressed the evils of an actor indicating on stage, it might now seem contradictory for me to state that indicating has a definite value in acting. But such is the case so long as it is restricted to rehearsals *only*.

During rehearsals indicating can be most useful to actors and directors alike and at times should be encouraged, primarily by the director. The purpose served by indicating at rehearsals is that it serves as a ''clearing shed'' for the truth. The director can sometimes acquire a clearer aspect of his actors' limitations in relation to their roles. For the actor it is useful when combined with imaginative processes of improvisation. This will be elaborated on later, but it should be considered most important how to realize that often in difficult roles a truthful medium can be obtained by indicating to the point of being "hammy." Whether certain actors in a scene are indicating or just a single actor, is left to the need of the scene by the director's discretion. He may suggest that they raise their voices, make every movement a flourishing gesture, and outwardly exaggerate every emotional expression. When indication is used to this extent, many of the realities and relationships of the character being portrayed can be expected to vanish, but other helpful results will remain to be added to the finished product. You will learn how much energy to use during the performance; the extent of your feelings, temperament, and imagination. The strength of a scene and possibly the play may depend on this.

True, anything is legitimate during a rehearsal, but the director must not make the mistake of allowing these indicating-rehearsals to progress or carry over into a normal rehearsal. It is the contrast of the normal rehearsal and the indicating one that helps to solve the problems which exist. It is interesting to note that mature actors have a stronger tendency to indicate their roles than beginners. He realizes that the audience's attention is often centered on the more emotional aspects of a role and he will attempt to gain this attention by indicating if he cannot create the inner truths of his role that would, in turn, produce the emotion truthfully.

The next problem is that of *imitating* and the stressing of certain habits that have been a bane to creative talent for generations. Most of these habits, because of a dearth of thought and expression in theatrical literature whose purpose is to seek truth instead of spectacle, have progressed into a jumble of bewilderment and misunderstanding. The "habits" connected with imitating must not be confused with the actor's natural tendency toward imagination because the latter's primary purpose is that of originality.

Imitating can be roughly divided into three groups: imitating can be an individual who is purely a product of the actor's imagination; imitating a real person who the actor decides is the kind of character his role calls for; imitating the personal characteristics and mannerisms of another actor.

The word imitation is an antithesis to originality, creativity, and reality. There cannot be imitation on stage and the presence of life, truth, and reality at the same time.

An actor usually begins his career by impersonating a semblance of a character instead of trying to live as a real person on stage. This is the case because of a lack of sympathy, knowledge, and training on his part. The actor who draws an image of his character in his mind and then sets about to imitate this behavior in a way contrary to his own instrument gets results in the shabbiest of characterizations. However, if he draws these same images that are purely imaginary and proceeds to adapt them to what is real in his own psyche and instrument, his character will be very much alive and expressive of truth on stage. Also, originality and creative spirit will result.

The reader may now ask why the actor cannot copy a person from real life and then impersonate him on stage; say, someone he has known for years and who he decides is just the sort of character the script calls for. The answer to this is that he can if he does not work for the end result first. The end result in this case would be a direct imitation of the person he knows in real life. He must first realize that he can never really become the person but, instead, can create the same qualities of the person which will apply directly to his characterization. To do this, he must use his own body and his own emotions to express the character, thereby making him real.

And what happens if we work for the end result first; that is, a direct imitation of the real person with whom we are familiar without creating the motivations for his behavior?

It is not difficult to imagine the results for we see them all too often. The character will resemble a crudely drawn caricature instead of the fine piece of art which could have been created. His speech will be mimetic instead of natural, his gait and general movement will be exaggerated.

In a biographical characterization of a real person whose personal mannerisms are known to the public at large, a great deal might depend upon makeup. Most important will be the actor's use of himself completely. He must let the figure flow through his instrument by way of his own emotions and movements, not trying to force his instrument to respond to a foreign image or element dictated by a cliche representation.

The third type of imitation which has come to us throughout the history of dramatic theatre is that of copying or imitating a fellow actor. This peculiar phenomenon, whether subconsciously or consciously done, should be considered a complete negation of the actor's purpose in life. Is not his purpose more than to just earn a living? Does not art, creativity, and personal expression enter into the picture?

It is possible through constant association on stage of a forceful and attractive personality that certain qualities typical of that actor might rub off onto another. Some of the qualities might be good, some bad. The danger, however, lies in the similarity which is more often than not discernible by the public. Some actors will subconsciously adopt the style of another, because of a deep-set admiration and a wish to be like him. Others will purposely copy for more mundane reasons such as publicity and associated trivia. Many actresses in the last decade have dressed, posed, and generally behaved like Marilyn Monroe in order to further their careers.

I suppose there have always been up-and-coming young actors to be touted by enterprising theatrical agents as the "new Kean" or the "new Edwin Booth," right up to modern times where many actors have had the experience of hearing their agents try to sell them as the "new Jimmy Dean."

The case of James Dean, that sensitive soul whose memory lives on due more to weird cults and teenage fan clubs than to a clear picture of creative talent, is an interesting example of how complex the problem of copying can become. Knowing his sensitivity and somewhat unusual powers of concentration, it has always remained a mystery to me how, or rather why, he let his talent become enshrined, or maybe I should say entombed, with another actor's style, even one as great as Marlon Brando.

Dean's personal admiration for Brando was well known in the theatre world and it manifested itself in his private life as well as in front of the camera. I remember only too well when the film "The Wild Ones" opened in New York. Several days after its opening, Jimmy bought a motorcycle, leather jacket, riding cap, and boots. He could on numerous occasions be seen in dingy Greenwich Village Bars, huddled off alone in a corner, sullenly sipping a bottle of beer. This is but one example of the bizarre and irrational proportions taken by his idolization of not only Brando, but even the characters he portrayed.

Now this is not to say that his own qualities never emerged, for they often did. These were the times that his acting held its most appeal. There were other times that an intermingling of the two forces would emerge. At these times a jerkiness in his movement and speech (in complete discordance with the reality of the scene he was playing) would occur. At the height of his career, this discordancy, which finally evolved into his own "style," was taken by a large portion of the public to be original, natural acting. Nothing could be further from reality for at this time the *real* James Dean rarely, if ever, allowed himself to be seen. Nor was Jimmy unaware of this. Indeed, his chagrin was brought to the surface when the movie version of John Steinbeck's novel *East of Eden* was reviewed by the *New York Times*. Their usually inane reviewer, Bosley Crowther, for once wrote a critique worthy of his profession and blasted Dean's performance for all it was worth. Dean came back to class for advice, but his future existence and work proved that he had not heeded it, for by that time a composite of two acting personalities had formed into one.

Another interesting mien of James Dean is that at the beginning of his career his acting and his personality were truly fresh and original. His early work on the New York stage and on television showed none of the imitation he later incorporated into his work. I personally like to believe that if he had not met his tragic death when he did, he would have eventually grown out of a temporarily immature phase of life and, perhaps, gone on to give the theatre a Hamlet to be remembered for generations to come.

So, as you see, it is better to create your own reality from what nature has given you than to copy the mannerisms and methods of another. When we do, we tend to copy just his style, his trademark. This alone is worthless without imitating his talent and this is impossible to imitate.

I have mentioned before the many facets of Stanislavsky's System of acting that seem no longer to have a practical purpose for the Western actor, at least in their original form. The reasons are the differences in production methods, length of time devoted to actors' training and training facilities. Mainly, the reasons boil down to the social differences between the governments of the U.S.S.R. and the U.S.A. The Russian theatre has always afforded a more scholarly existence for its actors by supporting them in the study and time needed to learn their craft. Conversely, the Western world for centuries has had a somewhat condescending view of actors and the theatre in general, which still exists to a large degree, and has stressed the actor's independence to succeed in the theatre in whatever way he may. The result being that the Western actor usually has a rather difficult time of it and, true to the tradition of free enterprise, finds himself seldom coddled in his ambition but nearly always having to claw himself to the top of the heap.

Several facets of Stanislavsky's System involved lengthy and time-consuming problems of rhythm, tempo, beats, speech control, movement, plasticity, and many more. Accompanying these problems were dozens of exercises used to assure the actor of complete naturalness on stage. Now, it may be that Westerners, Americans particularly, are just a bit more gregarious and ''naturally'' natural than the Russians were when Stanislavsky developed his system. At any rate, severe modifications have been found to be very adaptable and equally useful to us. Whereas the original system would have tied up our actors in endless controversies ranging from semantics to politics, the Method as we know it now can assist the Western actor to attain a hitherto unknown sense of reality. Because of the differences in casting procedures between the two countries, it is doubtful that the Russian actor ever had to submit himself to the system of "making the rounds" for work as the New York actor does. For the reader who does not know the term "making the rounds," it means walking to and from as many agents, producers, or general places of theatrical employment as possible between the hours of 10 A.M. to 5 P.M. five days a week, and then ninety-nine percent of the time returning home without a job.

Consequently, when the actor does get that rare chance for a job, which usually presents itself in the form of a "reading," it is easy to understand the added anxiety associated with this event because he usually gets one chance only at a reading. So, this problem created by our free society was found to contain related problems whose solutions can be utilized not only during the "first reading," but in first rehearsals and in finished productions as well. The related chapters on relaxation and concentration can be of great service during first readings. Under the circumstances, relaxation in giving credibility to your emotions and concentration in giving credence to the script are most important.

During a first reading the actor should try for the simple truths that lie in the author's words, not concerning himself with trying to create the character. In the first place he is usually given a short time (sometimes as little as half an hour, sometimes even less) to read over his part. Simple truths and, occasionally, a small facet of the role's character are the most that can be achieved at a first reading. For a perceptive casting agent, this is enough to stimulate his interest to progress you further in securing the role. Rarely can an actor approach a first reading with a full characterization present. But sometimes an actor is cast into a role by virtue of having done just this, only to have the director find out that the reading he saw was the extent of the actor's capabilities (usually quite stilted and artificial in scope). In other words, *his reading was his finished performance*.

The necessity for natural speech is very great during a first reading. When speaking to another person in life, we never know what the other person is going to say. Therefore, we do not know how, or what, we will answer. On stage we *do* know the other person's words and, also, our own lines. For this reason we must concern ourselves with having to speak naturally.

At first readings, as well as in performances, we must take care to try to communicate with our partner. You must speak to him as you do in life. You must make him understand you and, by so doing, you will be understood all the more.

So, if in life our dialogue is not planned, we are not able to *anticipate* the words we are going to say because much depends on the other person's verbalization. This is how it must be on stage. We must be careful not to anticipate what our partner is going to say even though we know his lines. To do so gives the slick gloss of artificiality to our meanings which is never really believable to the audience. An example of this is the slick, polished British style of repartee in their acting that is, at long last, becoming rather world-weary and vapid to all. Such a basic reality as natural simplicity in the first reading of an author's lines has won many a role.

Nor is anticipation an evil that is limited to speech alone. It should be guarded against in every phase of acting. Any bit of stage business, actions or movements, should be consciously worked on so as to appear fresh and natural at every performance. It is very disappointing to see one actor react to another mechanically in a way we can see was rehearsed constantly without the leeway afforded in life for a slightly different type of behavior.

Another aid to natural speech found useful in first readings, rehearsals, and eventually, in the performance is punctuation or, rather, the lack of punctuation. Actors tend to punctuate their sentences verbally exactly the way the lines were punctuated by the author. Grammatical laws with all their commas, periods, exclamation points, and question marks are observed as though they were being recited in a grammar school rhetoric contest. This is not done in life. Natural speech knows no punctuation. During first readings, the actor should make careful note of the lines and disregard punctuation, asking himself how he would say the lines if speaking them in life. It is at this point that he must have his fair share of actor's faith that the originality and truth of his expression will serve him best. It is this originality (this verbal expression as in life) that is sought by every playwright.

The objectivity needed in the study and preparation of lines can be aided by copying in longhand another set of the lines of the script. Only this time leave out all the punctuation including periods and commas. Let every line run into the succeeding one. This absence of punctuation will permit the actor to *see* his lines as they are spoken in life and, also, will help steer him away from setting verbal patterns in early rehearsals. Verbal patterns of speech are difficult to break once they have been set by several rehearsals. They hinder the actor from experimenting with improvisations which will produce varied realities, hence causing different readings of the lines. The more varied readings and interpretations the actor can create, the better his training is progressing. It is through improvisation that he can often find the reality he is seeking. Before advancing to another problem, let's discuss briefly how verbal patterns form traps for the actor when he memorizes his lines.

When given a part to portray, we quite naturally feel a certain pride in having been cast in the role and we often think of the role as "ours" alone. From the very first, we tend to feel an affinity for it. Because of this tendency, it is more often than not difficult to refrain from identifying ourselves with the lines immediately; that is, from the first rehearsals. Consequently, we begin to read the lines over, trying to memorize them, but subconsciously forming set patterns of how we will say them when on stage. This is the first step toward setting a verbal pattern which may be entirely wrong for the role and very difficult to break. Any kind of verbal pattern is destructive to an actor's originality. In life, we do not speak in verbal patterns but are, instead, led to speak by the forces around us which motivate our intonations, tempo of speech, and all the subtle nuances conveyed by speech.

Never worry about learning lines. They will come if the proper steps are taken. First of all, the actor should let the lines come to him instead of trying to force himself on the lines. By this I mean that he should use his script as often as necessary. This is its purpose. So many actors take pride in how quickly they can memorize their lines, as though they have accomplished a great feat. They have done nothing except put their preconceived ideas concerning the script into words and before rehearsals are concluded they usually find they have to abandon their ideas. When this happens, it in turn upsets their lines and makes them easy to forget. Does it not stand to reason that if an actor has decided beforehand how a line is to be read, it will be useless to work on the inner life which creates the motivation for saying the line? I repeat, in life we do not plan how we are going to speak. We speak in accordance with our feelings and situations.

If need be, the actor should improvise his own words frequently in the script during the rehearsals in order to get the feeling of how he would say the words in life. By creating different improvisational "realities," he will discover that the author's words will come to him quite naturally. They will be free and unstrained.

I once heard a Hollywood "star" expound on his way of "attacking" a role. (He is known for his screen aggressiveness.) First, he memorizes by rote every line of his part. This he does in two days. With the lines clearly out of the way (as though they are of secondary importance) he grabs the "meat" of the character, dons it physically (as though it were an old coat), tightens his jaws, bares his teeth ever so slightly, and, lastly, remembering the lines he so carefully learned, spouts them. Simple? Of course. Acting? Of course not.

The best formula to have when learning lines is one that is used throughout Method work: *Never Work First for the End Result*. (In this case, the lines of the play). Instead, first create the situations which will give meaning and life to the lines. In this way, the lines will be logical with what is occurring in the actor's inner life (his instrument) and will come automatically as the events in the play unfold.

It is my opinion that as Stanislavsky's method has progressed, there has been a definite relaxing of discipline regarding *physical control*. Stanislavsky always adhered to the old adage that actions speak louder than words, as did his immediate successors. They believed that physical movement and gestures should be kept to the barest minimum. Today, however, there are many professed teachers of the Method who stress complete freedom to the actor's impulses, off-stage as well as on-stage. In many cases, a freedom such as this can be good since it leads to the personal expression of the artist and ultimately to originality. But at other times it leads toward excessive self-indulgence which then moves toward conventional and cliché attitudes. The actor, his teacher, and the director must be aware of what is truthful and original in his every movement and, in many cases, for the good of the play, subordinate the actor to it. This probably sounds like a restriction of the actor's creativeness, but he must remember that what he creates is a segment in a play, not the play itself. This is the author's job.

During rehearsals, though, every effort should be made to permit full use of movement, good or bad, with the end result being the elimination of the bad (the cliche, the abject).

Presently, there is an actor on the New York stage who uses his hands for expression of everything he does on stage. He received acclaim by the critics in his first Broadway play some years ago for the "expressive use of his hands," and since that time has even increased their use on stage.

If this were his manner in life, thereby being an integral part of his own instrument, it might be artistically permissible. I know for a fact that it is not. Therefore, it is excessive and, instead, serves as a gimmick which he is fast coming to be known by. It is also becoming a crutch to express his emotions. This is not really an original manner of expression even though he does it with a certain flair not often seen in the theatre. The trouble with it is that after seeing this particular actor in two or three productions, you find yourself watching just his hands and wondering what he can possibly do with them next. The reason for this is that his hand movements are not in accord with the rest of his instrument. This is what makes them stand out. But because of the technique he has developed, even the astute observer is sometimes fooled. There seems to be a complete disharmony between his actions and what is going on in the play. It is this disharmony that really catches the eye of the beholder but it is his vast technique which holds it.

On the other hand, Miss Geraldine Page at first observation seems to possess a lack of physical control of voice and movement. In past years this was slightly distracting. It is only when the play unfolds, scene after scene, that the audience realizes that every gesture, word, movement, and flow of action forms a living, breathing human being on stage. Her seemingly disoriented physical control is such a sincere part of her instrument that everything she does is in direct accord with her characterization. If these were taken separately and attempted by another actor they would most surely appear as serious faults. With Miss Page, they only highlight the superior creative spirit dwelling within her. Hers is a perfectly integrated instrument with full expression of human frailties, in complete harmony with the character and the play. This is not to say she has not worked on this problem; for it is a problem, even though slight in her case. She has worked carefully on it with plenty of patience, foresight and, most important of all, understanding of the problem. By actually taking years to get a full awareness of what was happening to her when she was on stage, what needed to be done, and then setting about to correct it, always patiently, she ended up without disturbing her sensitive instrument at all. On the contrary, her acting talent is greater than ever before which shows she is still growing in her greatness as an actress. Geraldine Page is a living tribute to the art of acting and to the mountainous personal tasks which must be surmounted to reach true maturity.

Physical control is a problem that should be dealt with in a manner which stresses awareness on the part of actors, directors, and teachers. Exercises to correct this problem are ineffectual over a long period of time and the actor usually finds them to be too restrictive to his imagination. It seems, then, that an awareness of the problem is the answer and the conscious effort to set about correcting it through supervised scene work. For a profession that depends so much on mental work, it is a strange phenomenon that many actors will not stop and examine their own actions, not merely to intellectualize and justify their behavior but to correct it when necessary. Actors should learn, above all, that their art can best be served by their own awareness.

The presence in our theatre of diction and voice teachers who specialize in teaching actors how to speak, how to enunciate, or articulate in a dramatic and theatrical fashion, is indicative of the shallowness to which some factions of the theatre have succumbed. It is as though our actors are groping for a straw to cling to in a sea of perplexity concerning "acting technique through voice and diction."

These same teachers will attempt to teach an actor the "art" of learning to move, to walk on stage, and to coordinate each word with movement so that what comes out sounds and looks like only one step above a Charlie McCarthy.

Don't the teachers and actors realize that if they were unable to walk or talk, they never would have decided upon acting as a career? Don't they realize that you don't time or count steps in life when speaking? To do so on stage results in absolutely stilted behavior. These teachers of whom I speak try to mold each student into a particular model of speech and movement that is foreign to him, is unnatural to his behavior in life, never realizing that it is the behavior we possess in life that we should strive to perfect on stage. This is what forms our individuality and gives free vent to artistic expression.

With the exception of rare speech impediments or some physical malfunction, the vast majority of teachers who specialize in voice training are useless, indeed harmful to the actor for they tend to destroy his individuality. Even common speech traits such as regional accents are frowned on universally by voice teachers; traits which are a result of that individual's background and a vital part of the expression of his personality and charm.

Certainly, some heavy accents would be inappropriate for certain roles, but to try to do away with them completely can be a destructive influence.

Many diction teachers have concocted exercises which involve repeating words over and over again without any meaning, just for the express purpose of making sounds. This is definitely incorrect. The purpose of saying words is to convey inner emotions, thoughts, and feelings, not just to make sounds. Exercises such as these can do prodigious harm to the actor's instrument. The exercises are unnatural to speech and voice as we know them in life. In life, we speak to convey our inner selves and are innately aware of the vital link between our words and our emotions. This link can be damaged by the careless practice of repeating words in senseless exercises.

Certain speech patterns belonging to a certain actor (enunciations and accents included) have, because of their natural qualities, become as identifiable with that actor as his face. It is part of him; a part we know to be real.

I do not mean for this to sound like a diatribe against voice teachers with a desire on my part to see them put out of business. However, they should realize that their present methods of teaching are outmoded and useless to the actor. They should quit treating actor's voices and their speech as though they were mechanical puppets in a side show. Emphasis should not be placed on teaching an actor to act with his voice. It should instead be placed on making his voice flexibly adaptable so that is can impart the emotions of his instrument. Acting does not come from the voice. It comes from the inner life which the actor creates. The voice is a mere conveyance, a conductor of the emotions.

An actor should learn from his teacher how to strengthen the voice and how to develop the resonance of the voice. The teacher should be satisfied with teaching the student to speak distinctly without abolishing the personal characteristics of the voice. Many actors are bothered with the problem of a lack of resonance, not having the vibrant quality of tone needed to carry one's voice to the last row of a theatre. The truth is that the majority of people never realize the voice that nature intended for them to have. Reasons for this range from social inhibitions during childhood, when we were told by our elders how to speak, to just plain laziness in the application of our vocal machinery. The following exercise is used for the conscious strengthening of the voice. It is an excellent exercise designed strictly for improving the resonance. If it is done for ten minutes every day, the actor will soon be aware of a new power and intensification of tone that he never before possessed. The length of time for this change will vary with everyone, but it is usually noticeable after one or two months. I have seen this exercise deepen a man's voice, dropping it a full octave to his natural resonance.

If the voice becomes slightly hoarse after the exercise, there is no cause for worry. This is just a sign that the voice has not been used properly at the register and needs strengthening. You will find it very helpful and practical as it can be done in the privacy of your room.

EXERCISE I

(A) Stand up flat against a wall in your room with your hands at your side and your entire body from your heels to the back of your head touching the wall.

NOTE: The exercise simply consists of just moving the head slowly while counting out loud up to ten.

(B) Begin counting: one, two, etc., and as you count, slowly make the concentrated effort to touch the *back of the neck* to the wall. This will result in a slight tipping of the head for-

ward and a general pointing of the chin on the upper chest.
(C) As you count, use your *full* vocal strength to shout the
numbers as clearly and distinctly as possible and start with
the head level and eyes directly ahead.

> NOTE: It is probable that the back of your neck will never fully
> touch the wall as mentioned (B). This is not necessary; only the
> effort to do so, figuratively speaking, is necessary.

(D) Do this exercise as many times as you can in ten minutes
time, always remembering to raise the head to a level position before starting again. It is very important not to miss a
single day of doing the exercise, until the voice is where the
actor desires it to be.

The same outmoded methods of teaching diction and voice
are also prevalent among the teachers who include body work
in their indoctrinations. Also, the problems are similar to
those of voice and speech instruction. Where emphasis
should be placed on creating a supple, compliant, flexible
body full of natural expressiveness, teachers tend to train
bodies toward stylized representation and "dramatic" movement. The theatre demands much more than this. In the first
place, life itself is a drama and nothing can be more "dramatic" than its occurrences. This we know from just picking
up a newspaper and reading the headlines. Does it not then
seem logical that emphasis should be placed on body movement which is natural and free from any artificial theatricality
in order to create drama from life as it really is?

Whereas the actor should learn to speak simply, humbly,
and truthfully, instead of with vocal pathos and verbal gym-
nastics, he should also learn movement that has an actual
existence in life. This is something we should really not have
to learn since we do it every day of our lives. But for some
strange reason actors have a tendency to create a movement
which to their way of thinking is more theatrical than reality.
This is their biggest mistake. It is only when the audience
sees an ensemble of speech, movement, or behavior that they
can identify and associate in a personal way with their own
lives do they give that actor their undivided respect and attention. Of course, combined with these elements of natu-

ralness there must be the innate talent, sensitivity, poise, charm, and sometimes physical attractiveness to gain that respect. But if the actor is first unable to be accepted by the audience as a real person, the latter aspects of his talent will stand alone as merely superficial and conventional theatrics.

There are no known exercises taught in a classroom today that are helpful to the actor in learning natural movement on stage. I might even go further by saying that body movement exercises dictated from preconceived concepts are very detrimental to the actor because of the stylized molds they force upon him. Again, the answer lies a great deal within his own awareness of what is real and what is unreal.

The American stage is demanding of its actors and these demands increase with every season. I would recommend that the modern actor be not concerned with learning stage movement, body movement, and all of its associated trivia, but, instead, concern himself with building a strong, healthy body, one that is supple, flexible, and will respond easily to the will of the actor. Any study of "dramatic movement" cannot be worked on consciously or directly as this would be a classic example of working for the *end result* first, which without the inherent formation of the individuality of the actor, will seem stilted and artificial. Dramatic movement can only come about from the natural influences that compose it. Therefore, physical activity native to the actor's background must not be shunted aside and forgotten but, instead, should be encouraged and augmented. Even alien activities not necessarily taught in a formal classroom such as square dancing or Greek handkerchief dancing can add greatly to the composite development of natural stage movement. So, in addition to needing an awareness of the problem, there is also the activity derived from movement that is done in life, natural expressive movement. Any forms of physical activity that do not tend to mold the actor to a set pattern are of great value to him. How many times have we seen ballet dancers, desirous of acting careers, refused work because of their out-turned toes and undisguisedly trained posture? It is understandable that a walk resulting from many years of ballet training would be unsuitable for many acting roles, but I use this simply to point out the extremity of certain types of physical activity and the resultant dangers. A varied program of physical activity is very desirable in the actor's training. It is this variety, and the experience gleaned from it, that produces a body ideally suited for the theatre, a body simple and natural in movement and yet completely free and strong. When these natural processes have been attained, the body then and only then, will be able to produce the dramatic effect of reality sought by the actor.

The last two acting problems to be discussed in this chapter will be centered around the exercises used to solve them. These exercises, one for each of the two problems, cannot be done by the actor alone. The two exercises I describe and explain can only be effective in a classroom under the expert supervision of a qualified teacher. Also, the presence of a class of students is equally necessary to the awareness of the actor doing the exercises. This I shall explain as we go along.

The first exercise is called a *Singing Exercise*, but do not let this title deceive you as the exercise is not intended as an aid to singers or even for the voice proper. Occasionally, however, rare cases of tone deafness will be discovered through the exercise and can even be remedied by its continued application. The exercise is always done as the second half of the classwork Sense Memory Exercises covered in Chapter Three, always following the Sense Memory work. Of course, the Singing Exercise can be done by itself since the Sense Memory Exercise is in no way related to it, but the Singing Exercise itself is divided into two parts with the second half of it being rather strenuous. Therefore, it is better to precede it with any Sense Memory Exercises planned for the student's day.

The purposes of the first half of the Singing Exercise are many. It is one of the perplexities of the acting teacher that there are problems innate with actors that are very elusive and, at times, intangible. These problems often include a mental block against expressing, in front of an audience, strong emotions such as tears; hence, the usefulness of the class. The problems may be those of nervous mannerisms, cliche expressiveness, bashfulness, and literally dozens more. The exercise, if supervised correctly, will expose many problems the actor could never have solved alone and many he probably never knew he had.

You will notice throughout this book the usage of words, terms, and phrases which may seem to be repetitious at first; phrases like "Never work for the end result," "Just make the effort" to do so. There is a reason for this which boils down to the fact that the terminology was instilled in me over such a long period of time by my teacher due to the importance and emphasis to be placed on them. The same holds true for the reader.

In working on the first part of the Singing Exercise, another term of direction I shall stress is, *Do Not Sing the Song with Any Preconceived Meaning*. You must remember that the purpose of the exercise is for an aid to freeing the instrument and not that of seeing how well the song can be sung in a conventional sense. The first half of the Singing Exercise should be conducted as follows:

The actor must pick a simple song he knows well. He must stand in front of the class and sing the song, carrying the basic melody throughout, but with a complete absence of trying to "put the song across." This means no arm movements or excessive facial movement such as the raising of eyebrows and, most important, no vocal intonations that suggest the meaning of the song's lines or story. The actor's eyes and full attention must be on the class of students.

The purpose in staying away from singing the song with its meaning is: Because we may hear a song on a recording, radio, television, nightclubs, or movies, we tend to "sing along" with the music or the vocalist and consequently fall into a *vocal pattern* of singing. This vocal pattern, if allowed in the exercise, can be used as a cloak to hide the emotions and true feelings that are going on inside the actor's instrument while he does the Singing Exercise. The main purpose of this portion of the Exercise is to make the actor aware of what is happening to him *inside* as he sings the song. The song acts solely as a primer and a conveyor of the emotions just as a bucket of water is needed to start a hand-pumped well. He must examine his emotions personally as they occur and allow them to pour forth from his instrument whether they be anger, tears, laughter, or even indifference. Emotions of some kind are going on inside of all of us at all times and while doing the exercise the song must not be stopped for any reason until the teacher thinks the fullest point has been reached.

The actor, on the first attempt of the exercise, frequently shows anxiety due to the first signs of awareness of his voice and feelings as they occur. It sometimes helps for his teacher to allay his anxiety and, also, to prevent his trying to escape this super-consciousness by telling him not to worry and by explaining to the whole class the beauty of the pure emotion being released. In this way, the class and the student can observe what is taking place in an almost impersonal manner. The actor doing the exercise should make the effort to relax during the exercise in order to allow the emotion to flow forth. This will also let him make an easier examination of what is happening.

For some unknown reason, tears are the most frequent strong emotion which is released. This is good, very good, for tears and their expression are often the result of an unknown mental block that has been removed, one that could obstruct the instrument in actual stage work.

This exercise, if supervised and done properly by the actor, can be the most beneficial of all his work in a class. Because of its partisan nature in relation to the actor's inner self, the results are automatically carried over into his preparatory work, and final stage work.

It is interesting to note that this first half of the Singing Exercise has no strict counterpart in any of Stanislavsky's work. Stanislavsky used many methods of improvisation which incorporated super-awareness; exercises that were designed to explore the emotions and free them, but only in relation to actual roles being rehearsed for class work or production. The Singing Exercise which was developed in

America as we know it today includes much of his technique and is certainly pure Stanislavsky method in principle. It is but another example of the Western theatre's way of going directly to a problem and solving it. This has, of course, been through sheer necessity as our productions and training do not allow time for an overabundance of circumspection.

The second half of the Singing Exercise is extremely useful in finding and rooting out inhibitory qualities present in the actor's body and voice. These inhibitions that manifest themselves so secretly cannot be observed by oneself and, again, it takes a discerning teacher to present them to the actor. It is then up to the actor to destroy them.

This part of the exercise should immediately follow the first half. In it the student sets himself a series of physical movements while he sings the song. The movements must be determined, forceful, exertive, and varied. A typical series of movements would be to set a march step around the stage, change to a skip, then, standing still, move the torso in a controlled but free and rhythmic jazz, going from one step to another without a break in between. He must sing the song all the while he goes from one change to another, only it is really not singing. The voice must be projected from the chest with all the force at his command, forcing each word or part of a word out in a sudden and dynamic burst of sound. The purpose is to let the voice flow out of the movement, not to try to make it accompany the movement. This exercise will display to the class the problems involved in true expressiveness; the natural relationship between our actions and the spoken word. The class, the teacher, and the actor doing the exercise will discover many cases of repressed movements and repressed sounds of the voice; sounds which stay hidden deep in the chest until given the opportunity to be released. This exercise will be the answer to many similar intangible acting problems as well.

The last problem and its associated exercise, called a *Private Moment*, concerns the difficulty we all have in trying to behave on stage exactly as we would at home under the same conditions. This problem deals with inhibitory factors too, as will be seen.

When we are in the privacy of our own room, we behave in a way known only to us. We behave this way because of the knowledge that we are alone and unobserved. We sit a certain way in privacy that we might not sit if there were but one other person in the room. We may sing in a way we would never sing in front of an audience. We may do all sorts of menial tasks in a completely different way if we know that we are being observed. In privacy we show the truth. This is our real self. This is the behavior and these are the things that we want to see on the stage.

A Private Moment is an advanced type of exercise and a great amount of concentration and relaxation is needed. Not surprisingly, it is rarely a complete success after only several attempts. The reason being that the actor chooses a moment, a private one in his own personal life, and then presents it intact for the class. All of his earlier training of concentration, will, Sense Memory, and relaxation must be utilized if the following-through of the Private Moment is done with the knowledge of full observation by the class. I have seen Private Moments that might seem embarrassing to describe were it not for the beauty of the actor's freedom as it led the beholder away from the obvious to the full expanse of originality.

Another class exercise associated with the problem of reaching the inner self and releasing it in front of an audience is called a *Monologue*. A Monologue is used primarily in rejecting the verbal meaning of the lines. In it the actor memorizes a conversational monologue as though he were speaking to someone. He must not express emotionally any of the lines which do not mean anything to him. He must sit on the stage and speak to the class, remembering that the lines have no real meaning to him as a real human being. You would be surprised to note how difficult it is to speak the lines simply and without any meaning at all. The exercise will point out the habits we pick up in life of expressing words we do not really feel, words we do not really mean. During this exercise, the teacher should ask the actor if such and such a work has any real meaning to him just to point out to him the conventional emotional speaking habits he has adopted.

This chapter began with the problem most associated with Method actors: that of too much intellectualizing. Perhaps the reader will feel that to intellectualize is necessary or maybe that it is a problem within a problem. We shall never know. Certainly, we can not be led by blind intuition. Also, we know it is possible to become effete with too much theory and not enough practice. Then where does the answer lie in regard to too much intellectualization? I cannot answer this for it lies with each individual's awareness. If there is an answer, then awareness is the secret to it. Awareness is the greatest part of the actor's intellect. This he must develop; this he must use to serve his talent, his artistry, for this is sometimes all he has and it is everything.

Improvisation

It is a sad plight of the Western theatre that, generally speaking, most theatre productions eliminate improvisation as a fundamental aspect of a play's rehearsal. Not nearly enough importance is given to improvisations in this country.

In the early years of the Moscow Art Theatre as much time as was deemed necessary (usually several weeks, sometimes even months) was devoted to familiarizing the actors with their roles through individual and ensemble improvisation. This practice has been maintained from the beginning and the results are well-known. The artistic and public acclaim of the Moscow Art Theatre has never diminished.

Present day directors and producers in this country are almost as a whole disdainful of improvisational methods because of the extra time they absorb. The budget of a play sometimes will not allow for the extra weeks needed for this purpose and, consequently, a most integral part of the Method, to say nothing of the play's production standard, is lost. Only a handful of modern directors today will insist on and emphasize the inclusion of improvisations for their rehearsals. Elia Kazan, Harold Clurman, Jack Garfein, and Frank Corsaro are well-known for their strict adherence to this all-important phase of the Method.

Many conscientious actors are forced to get together on their own time, after a rehearsal and improvise their scenes away from a scornful director. This is an admirable trait on the actors' parts and shows a true dedication to their art that commercialized theatre cannot destroy. But, it certainly does not speak too highly of the circumstances which prompt such action. The situation as presented does not in any way detract from the deplorable lack of insight on the part of certain directors. True, improvisations take up valuable rehearsal time but the knowledge to be found, the insight, the familiarization with a role, and the freshness acquired are even more valuable than the time spent. How can an actor be expected to slip into a role without proper familiarization with the complexities associated with many dramas? If one has never before bought a pair of gloves, one cannot order by size, but, instead, must try them on. So it is with a role, indeed sometimes with every role in a play. This is where improvisation comes in.

To begin with, there are many forms and shapes that improvisations can take, but for the modern actor and director these are generally grouped into two distinct types. The first is for the actors and director to choose circumstances that are similar but not the same as the situations in the play. An example of this would be in the role of the holdout juror (juror No. 8), in Reginald Rose's *Twelve Angry Men* who from the very beginning of the play maintains a Not Guilty verdict for the defendant, a young Puerto Rican product of New York's slums, charged with murdering his own father. Juror No. 8's Not Guilty ballot is in direct opposition to the other eleven jurors, who for reasons ranging from racial prejudice to circumstantial evidence, have from the beginning cast their juror's ballots for a Guilty verdict. It is for the obvious reasons that juror No. 8 holds out with his vote to gain time in an attempt to at least discuss the case at some little length in the confines of the jury room. He feels that the defendant's life is at stake, which it surely is, and such a quick verdict of Guilty with such flimsy evidence is more or less arbitrary.

Now, to improvise the opening scenes of the play, a premise quite different can be taken by the actor playing juror No. 8. He can take, as an example, purely selfish motives for his withholding a Guilty vote instead of the noble ones presented by the author. When these selfish motives are created by the author (and they can be varied and be made personal) an entirely different situation will unfold on stage. The action of the improvisation will remain the same as the play, as will the lines, but the actor will find that his lines will take on different meanings. Because he has created a situation in his imagination, one that the other actors are not informed of beforehand, he is forced by the improvisational situation to speak, to move, and to listen in accordance with it. Out of this will come lines that do not sound memorized. The same result will be true with the other actors in the scene. They will be forced to reply in a fresh and natural way to the new reality of the scene. This type of improvisation is very useful in exposing lack of concentration and illogical thinking processes on the part of the actors involved.

The second type of improvisation has to do with the actors continuing the logical sequence of events and the actual meaning of the play as set down by the author. But instead of using the author's words, the actors must substitute their own words. This type of improvisation is usually done after the play has been read through several times, the author's interpretation has been fully explained and understood by the actors, and, also before the actual lines of the play have been memorized. Because each actor is speaking his own words, his partner will be forced to listen just as he does in life. He will not be simply waiting for a cue. In this way he will become closely involved with the true meaning of the play and will in turn find that the author's lines come to *him* in a natural way, not through the pure necessity of having to memorize them.

Other interesting and useful improvisations can be done by improvising different settings, or locales, for your scenes. For instance, suppose a script calls for a scene to take place in a barn late at night but for some reason as the scene unfolds, it does not quite possess the quality desired by the director and expressed by the author. The quiet of night and the stillness of a barn at that hour are all lacking in the scene.

Now suppose the scene were improvised as taking place

in a cemetery and the actors are compelled to visualize the interior of their "barn" set as a portion of the graveyard. Imagine the stillness that would come over the scene, the extreme awareness of sounds; those strange sounds of animals unseen, moving in their stalls, and the reaction of the actors to them as their concentration remained on their imaginary locale, the cemetery. An improvisation such as this might prove to contain just the eerie quality of night sought by the director. For anyone having experienced the sensation of entering a deserted building, barn, or similarly unfrequented place at night will no doubt recall the similarity between it and a graveyard. One "sense" that can come out of it is that these kinds of places are not as quiet as we think they are. There are many night noises which can develop in an improvisation like this one.

For strange effects and extraordinary combinations, we must go to life itself which is always far more daring than any effort of theatrical surrogates. And it is through improvisation that billiant reasoning power can be made to rise to the level of pure artistic intuition.

During these improvisations the actor's actions, inflections, and impulses that arise spontaneously should be carefully noted and encouraged. These impulses are often the freshest aspects of an interpretation and should be developed with the thought of incorporating them into the play.

A rather humorous incident regarding improvisations was told to me by the actress-wife of a now well-known stage and movie director who, at the time, was quite unknown and was just beginning his directorial studies with Lee Strasberg. This budding director had heard somewhere that Chekhov's *Three Sisters* was Lee Strasberg's favorite play. With the hope of pleasing his new teacher, he chose a scene from this beautiful play to direct and present as his introductory scene in the class.

Somewhere along the line he remembered hearing Strasberg lament on the fact that many directors unfamiliar with Chekhov miss a great deal of the humor inherent in Chekhov's style of writing. He then chose the actresses from class that he wanted to play the Prozorov sisters for a scene to last almost thirty minutes. He rehearsed them assiduously. During these rehearsals, the course of improvisations took place. Evidently, they not only took place, they must have taken over. For when the scene was presented in Strasberg's direction class, it opened with one of the sisters sitting at a table hungrily devouring an Italian Hero sandwich; another was sitting cross-legged in a great overstuffed chair nonchalantly puffing away on a big black cigar. The third sister was standing in front of a full-length mirror, trying on a big, floppy black hat and doing ballet positions called pliés.

No one heard more than the opening lines due to the hysterical laughter by the class. Everyone laughed, it seems, except Strasberg who at the conclusion managed to ask the "director" what he had worked for in directing the scene.

"Humor," he replied quite seriously to a classroom that immediately fell to pieces once again. Strasberg's only comment was, "That will be all. Next scene, please." Strasberg's criticisms are always erudite and lengthy, but not that day. I do believe that for once in his life he was stunned by the work done in class.

This story is humorous in its proper perspective, but I am sure the scene served as a good example to the class as a whole without Strasberg condescending to offer an obvious criticism. For while it undoubtedly showed great imagination and freedom on the part of the director, it also pointed out to an extreme degree how improvisations must not be allowed to carry over into the proper perspective of the play as set down by the author. In this case, the director's imagination promoted his failure because the results he obtained were the acknowledgement of defeat in his clash with the reality of Chekhov's interpretation.

Rarely does an author enjoy having his play trifled with, especially with regard to content and interpretation. However, a play that was written almost in its entirety through improvisation is Michael Gazzo's *Hatful of Rain*. *Hatful of Rain* is something of a phenomenon with regard to the formula for playwriting and I use it only to point out one of the many creative results obtainable from improvisation. Originally written as a half-hour acting scene intended for class work in an Actors Studio project, it was improvised, discussed, written a little, expanded, improvised, and rewritten by the actors until a three-act play emerged through imaginary situations created by the actors and Gazzo. Gazzo's astute observations as actor turned teacher turned playwright truly produced an excellent script. It is interesting to note that subsequent attempts at playwriting have not yielded Mr. Gazzo the *success d'estime litteraire* he enjoyed with "Hatful."

Mike Nichols began his career as a serious drama student who surmounted many obstacles just to continue his studies in acting. But it was by improvising whimsical studies of life with an equally talented young actress named Elaine May that gave rise to the sequences for which both have gained stardom as brilliant comedians. Nor did they neglect improvisation as a fundamental part of their work. Every new comedy sequence is improvised many times, in many different ways, until the finished situation results.

Improvisation is granted by a talented few to be the most important part of a play's rehearsals. It serves to keep the bindings of theatrical conventionality, so difficult to break when formed, from even appearing and to lend the lifegiving freedom of personal expression to a role.

I can not urge actors strongly enough to grant themselves this freedom, to demand it if necessary.

Actors, theatrical conventionality will strangle your art. Art and freedom cannot exist without each other. The very soul of art demands freedom. For your freedom as artists, actors, *improvise!*

Justification

All the preparatory work for a role, physical and mental, must be governed by the same basic rules of nature that we experience from life. Feelings felt in life are the result of circumstances that have happened before, thus producing the feelings. They are never the result for their own sake. When a person feels pain from a burn, the pain is the result of the *fire*, not the *pain* itself. It is the circumstances that have happened before that we must create on stage and let the end results produce themselves.

When we are given physical actions to follow through on stage, even the simplest of tasks, there must be a purpose for them. All stage actions, behavior, and "business" must have a purpose. These tasks must be carried through to their logical conclusions truthfully.

In this chapter some of the natural laws and principles which preside over *Justification* and *Motivation* will be discussed. To begin with, if an actor is to convey his tasks to a logical, consistent, and realistic conclusion they must be "justified" by the tenets of the play as laid down by the author. By this I mean they must have *real* reasons, reasons that are real to the actor's instrument, and they must be justified for occurring as they do. These reasons are the actor's motivations. We must learn to act the *reasons* for a character's behavior.

In life we do not plan our emotional responses. Therefore, it is equally important to learn the art of forgetting the *end results* of a character's behavior, thus allowing the results to happen as they do in life. The simplest stage action must have purpose designed for its existence. Sitting in a chair on stage must have a purpose, a reason for it being done. And with this reason will come the naturalness and simplicity of the act. How many times have we seen an actor sitting on stage who looks as if he is sitting on a stage instead of behaving as he would in his own home, office, or club? You may now ask how can an action as singularly simple as sitting in a chair have any purpose other than the fact that the director placed him there. True, in its surface meaning, yet, in just such a simple action we see otherwise capable actors react unrealistically. Watch an actor sitting in a chair on stage and then watch a person in life sitting on a park bench. Will the actor possess the simplicity, the naturalness, the quiet vitality of his counterpart on the park bench? Usually not.

You may now say, "But the script and even the director tell me of no action, no clue to my behavior, other than that I am to sit in the chair." True, but this is where the actor's art comes in and it is then up to him to justify his task of simply sitting in a chair. This justification can be the result of his intellect, imagination, or awareness so long as there is a reason for it.

In life we sit in chairs to rest tired feet, to watch television, to read a book, eat meals, play cards, write letters, and a thousand other reasons, and out of these reasons come the truthful, natural behavior which we express in life. The actor can never say that he is sitting in a chair on stage because the director told him to do so. He may have to find his own reason, his own justification for doing so, but find one he must. All too often a director will overlook simple activities on the stage, thereby losing a great deal of reality that should be inherent in a scene. The actor must then deploy his imagination, his art.

The traveling companies of the Moscow Art Theatre in the 1920's and 1930's were especially acclaimed for their supernumeraries. This was expressed even in crowd scenes. Critics of the day exclaimed that each and every actor-extra in a crowd scene seemed to be thoroughly absorbed into the action of the play while, at the same time, possessing extraordinary individuality; a complete life of his own, interesting, varied, and easily discernable to the audience. How refreshing this would be today. Too many directors form their "supers" into a jumbled mass of humanity, hardly realizing how really important a crowd scene can be to the over-all stage effect. Of course, many stage directors do realize the importance of the extra but still do not have the ability to do anything about it. Many directors are deeply afraid of staging crowd scenes and shy away from the responsibility. For some reason, their imaginations disappear when they have to create a crowd ensemble on stage.

It is when we can justify our activity on stage, as easily as the person sitting on a park bench expresses his, that we reach the heights of our art, whether we be "star" or "super." It is natural to assume that consanguinity for a character's motivations often leads to an easier justification. This affinity for a role may be conscious or unconscious on the actor's part. It really does not matter as it is rarely distinguishable to him. Ask any great actor at various times during the stages of a rehearsal how he feels in his part. Usually his feelings are in direct contrast to the reaction of the observer.

Lee J. Cobb was once queried when he was rehearsing Arthur Miller's *Death Of A Salesman* as to how he thought he had just done in a scene. He replied that he felt he had held his characterization throughout and expressed his emotions with a maximum of verisimilitude. Since the person who was asking was a very close friend, and he held this friend's opinion in the highest respect, Mr. Cobb was quite startled when told that he was straining for his emotions, had not an iota of the character during the scene, and was generally not believable even in the simpler moments of the scene.

In a few minutes the scene was run through again. When he came offstage this time, he said to his friend that he thought he must have done quite badly for he didn't even remember much of what he had done. Imagine his astonishment now when he was informed that he had done beautifully. He was told that he had completely assimilated the character through his own instrument, had expressed real emotions, was simple, natural, completely life-like, and thereby thoroughly believable.

This result may at first seem strange until examined a little closer. What happened during the first rehearsal was a conscious affinity for the character, but expressed only mentally to himself with the belief that this would lead to the characterization. Later, at the second rehearsal, he unconsciously felt the consanguinity for the character through his concentration on the tasks needed to create the characterization. Hence, the second rehearsal produced the desired results because his concentration did not allow him to think consciously of what he was doing but, instead, allowed him to work on his tasks and let the results take care of themselves.

After the scene was over, he could not remember all of what he had done or how he had said his lines because all of his effort was applied to the work, the task he had set for himself. This was why, at first, he thought he had done badly.

Justification is applied to every part of a play beginning first with the author's concept of the story line and continuing through to each actor's motivation for what he does on stage.

Stanislavsky built his system of justification around one word, IF. The actor, for instance, says, "If I were in this particular situation in real life, what would I do, what would I say, how would I say it, and why?" The answers to these questions lead the actor toward truthful stage results. For every question there may quite possibly be more than one truthful answer. It is then up to the actor and director to decide which of these factors is most suited to the play and to the actor's instrument. These different factors or circumstances of a situation are called *Adjustments*. These Adjustments involve the finer points of interpretation that lead to the highest development of the actor's art. The young actor will usually find that as his training progresses and his experiences enlarge, he will make Adjustments automatically in accordance with the author's interpretation.

Stanislavsky invented a series of exercises for outward justification that proved to be useful in his time. However, they have not proven to be very popular in this country as they are considered to be superfluous to the phases of the Method that are readily accepted for practical use. These exercises include striking any spontaneous physical pose with the body and then holding it in that position. While holding this position he examines the pose and seeks to justify exactly what he might be doing in life if he were in that particular position. For example, the actor strikes a pose with his hands flung high into the air or one with his arms outstretched to either side.

In one case he might justify the high flung arms and hands by actually trying to reach an imaginary object, say, on a shelf. In the other case he may be trying to span the width of a small room or he may even be trying to separate two fighters.

The pose itself, without the justification that follows, is nothing but a hollow gesture, false and without purpose, but as soon as a real motivation and justification is found, the exercise will have a reason for existing. It will have life. I know of only one Method teacher who uses this phase of Stanislavsky's system in her teaching. Her own method of teaching has always included the more physical and outward phases of his system, leaving the students to find their own way of working on the inner self.

Many teachers still attempt to teach Stanislavsky's IF system exactly on the basis that he taught it: Centered purely around the word IF as the sole justification for stage behavior. In Stanislavsky's time, actors may have been more apt to hit upon the reality of an imaginary situation than they are today by use of the IF, although I personally doubt this. The use of the IF is falling into desuetude among Stanislavsky's staunchest followers in this country. Possibly the reason for this is that too much supposition is connected with the word in the modern actor's mind thereby indicating frailty of human decision. Lee Strasberg included the IF Method in his teachings years ago, but rarely stresses its use now. Its use in his classes is left entirely up to the individual.

A search for justification is a search for the truth. An incident involving that great showman of the past, George M. Cohan, illustrates how an actor can find a task to lend interest to a scene, but then fails miserably to justify it being included at all, simply because if was an untruth.

The majority of the scores of plays that Cohan wrote, directed, and starred in were ultimate successes of the time. However, one in particular had a serious problem with the first act, especially the end of the first act. It was uneventful throughout, the ending seemed disjointed, did not seem to tie in with the two acts to follow, and was in short, sluggish, and boring. It was felt by the producer and the rest of the cast that the first act did not stimulate interest and would probably leave the audience with not the slightest desire to remain for the second and third acts, which were quite engaging and managed to culminate in a most exciting climax to the play. Today these last two acts would have probably assured the play's success even though Act One was dull. But in Cohan's day, with theatre tickets more moderately priced, the public had to be entertained in every act, especially the first, or else they would walk out.

Anyone who had anything to do with this particular play was noticeably concerned. Through all of their combined anxieties concerning the first act, Cohan remained calm and adamant about changing it, always giving his assurance that everything would be all right. Dress rehearsal came with no changes having been made. Everyone connected with the play thought they had a flop on their hands and were visibly upset. Opening night came and with it a cheery and optimistic George M. Cohan.

When the curtain opened on Act One, Cohan made his entrance in a scene which took place in a bedroom. He came into the room dressed in a very handsome dressing gown. From the pocket of this dressing gown he withdrew a small menacing looking revolver. Walking across the stage to a bureau, he opened a drawer, placed the gun inside, and then quietly closed the drawer. He then went about with the business of playing the first act.

Now, the cast had no inkling of the gun's significance, for indeed it had none, but a noticeable ripple of interest swept through the audience. The act was played through to the end with crashing applause. Needless to say, no one left the theatre and at the end of the act everyone was intent upon the mystery of the gun. It had lent the interest to hold the audience for the rest of the play, always promising more to come. Acts Two and Three were played to a rousing end, and, strangely enough, few members of the audience remembered the business of the gun at the final curtain. This is a classic example of a stage action being taken, but without a single shred of justification, save that of the producer's investment being protected. I imagine that to even the most vapid critic of the day, it seemed like not much more than a cheap theatrical trick.

We actors have come a long way since the time we were spat upon by the public at large and we must be careful to preserve what we have honestly striven for and attained. We have only in the last few years been recognized as artists in the true sense and for this recognition to have come about as belatedly as it has should impress upon us that it too had to have a justification. Let us make certain we do not lose it. Stage actions must not be done with a predetermined plan to please the audience for this would also be a case in point of working for the end result. When stage actions and spoken words are planned in advance, they lose their freshness and spontaneity. The audience may react to them, they may laugh, but they will never believe. They will say how similar he is to someone they know, when speaking of an actor's role, but they will never say that he was completely real to them. Every stage action, every word, every situation, and every task must be done because the actor believes it and because he has created his own truthful justification.

Imaginative Personalization and Substitution

The actor's imagination often serves as a gauge reflecting the degree of originality which he is able to bring to his role. It is the basis for all that is fresh, new, novel, young, and *original*. Imagination also serves as an uplifting balm to stifled creativity and is as vital to an actor as rosin is to a violinist's bow.

I have purposely avoided until now any full and interpretative examination of the many uses of the actor's imagination but, instead, have imparted briefly some of the many outside forces derived from an acute awareness to life (nature particularly) which stimulate and feed our imaginations. I then intentionally passed on to the subject already under discussion, probably leaving the vague feeling that imagination is something worthwhile to possess, even necessary for the artist, but perhaps slightly intangible regarding the aspect of its cultivation for acting purposes. But is imagination really so intangible and can it be cultivated or is it what we so often tend to think of it as: An indefinable source that lies deeply buried within ourselves, an innate part of our instrument and our talent, bursting forth from the sudden beck of inspiration only? Since inspiration is usually an all too rare occurrence that seems only to follow genius wherever it goes, we tend to think of constant imaginative powers as similarly akin to intangibles of that sort.

All too often actors sell themselves short for there are two important areas in acting where imagination is shown to be a most evident and palpable gift, attainable for all. In these two areas inspiration is reduced to its true nature; that of subconscious ideas and impulses not all dependable and rarely of use on stage except to produce an exceptionally good performance from an actor not capable of doing so without it. Also, in these areas the actor will discover that imaginative results occur not from "magical inspiration," but through the conscious effort of the individual.

The areas of most interest to the modern actor are the phases of the Method where these occur; where his imagination is not merely stimulated but actually created consciously to produce original and likely results. These phases or areas of the Method are called *Personalization* and *Substitution*.

In the first we recognize that there are experiences, relationships, involvements, desires, and situations arising in scripts that can best be expressed by finding a common ground with our own life's desires, relationships, and involvements. The actor will find a greater affinity for these circumstances within the role by a direct association of that circumstance which is real to him because it stems from his own life and the one present in the script. When he forms this direct association he is actually using his concentration and imagination to personalize them. Thereby, he makes them more dear to his sensibility, to his instrument as a whole, and, ultimately, to the audience.

The word personalize means "making personal" or "making familiar" to the sensitivity and to the awareness of the instrument. When he applies a Personalization, the actor soon finds that a greater amount of truth is rendered to his role than would be if the imagination were left to function alone with only a false premise to guide it. A false premise in this case would be the acceptance of the script's situation without a parallel situation from the actor's own life; one which would be appositely in accordance with the plot of the play. When one finds a similar incident or a relative truth or a familiar desire in his own life that correlates with the action and central theme of the play, he must use his concentration to replace mentally the author's situation with his own *real* situation. For if the situations or the character's desires mean nothing *personally* to the actor, how can he be expected to attain anything more than a superficial interpretation of the role, one that is augmented only by the hollowness of meaningless speeches and erroneous behavior?

Replacing these circumstances with Personalizations belonging to the actor are done more simply than Affective Memory exercises in that they usually require less concentrated effort. The main objective is to attain a parallel "feeling" or understanding of the circumstance in the script, one which the actor can relate to more directly with his whole instrument. It is this creation of a parallel experience from life, inserted into the role, that allows the actor to become closer to his role and the central theme of the play and, also, to become an integral part of the ensemble of actors on stage.

Personalizations are one phase of the Method where the necessity of building a sensory foundation is conspicuously absent with one exception: Unless the parallel personalization contains an outstanding sensory object important to its existence. An example of this would be, say, the loss of all one's material possessions through some disaster. Now, if the actor had actually suffered a similar experience in his past, perhaps the loss of all his furniture, clothes, etc., by a fire, then the *smell* of smoke and burning material may weigh heavily in his mind for years to come whenever he recalls the experience. In this case, the sense of smell or the sight of the flames will play an important part subconsciously in the coalescence of the real experience and the one in the script. Also, it is not difficult to realize that it would only be a short hop to a possible Affective Memory experience if the concentration were allowed to dwell excessively on the sensory aspects of the Personalization. For if it does, the actor may find himself bridled with an emotional aspect that has no basis in the script. On the other hand, it is possible that just the right amount of emotion is found to be useful. Naturally, it would depend entirely on the script and its needs for the Personalization.

However, it is important for the actor to realize that Personalizations usually are not expected to progress far emotionally. They should enable him to grasp familiarly the whole idea; the main ingredient of the situation in the play with an eye to understanding and closely relating to it.

As a simple illustration of how Personalization is used, let us suppose that a play's character is motivated in his behavior by an inalienable drive of one sort or another. Whether it be a thirst for alcohol, chasing women, a desire for material riches, or a taste for chocolates that manifests from the drive, let us assume that the actor portraying the role has nothing more than a normal, healthy attitude regarding the "object" (which to the character has taken on super-importance). Now, if the actor goes ahead and plays the role without first finding an emphatic relationship or understanding of his own to the problem of the character, the chances are great that he will never fully understand the character or his problem, and this fact can hardly escape the attention of the audience.

If the actor does not understand such a problem, what he must do is to stop and ask himself: "Where am I like the character? What likes, desires, drives, do I have that I could compare to his that might, if given free rein, carry me to the extremes that have carried my character in the play?"

It is this empathy in the actor's own personal make-up which corresponds to the circumstances in the play that must be found, for empathy is a strong basis for making something truly personal and real to you.

It is important for the reader to note that as the phases of the Method progress, there is a definite intertwining relationship between each phase which will become even more evident later in this chapter. This intertwining began with the fundamental use of Sense Memory in Chapter Three which then led directly to Affective Memory continuing through to the present chapter where the close relationship between Imaginative Personalization and Substitution are shown. This intertwining will also encompass all subsequent chapters. The reader should by now be getting a clearer picture of how the actor's imagination is actually being *trained* to function creatively and instinctively through the originality of his own life.

Whereas Personalizations embody the feeling and understanding of a character's particular involvement in the play, *Imaginative Substitutions* are concerned more closely with physical objects and, therefore, revert back to the Method's dependency on Sense Memory. However, even though a dependency on Sense Memory is inherent and isn't with Personalizations, the close association between Personalizations and Substitutions will be obvious.

An Imaginative Substitution is exactly what the name implies. It is a mental means whereby a stage property, an object or a situation, even another actor, can seemingly be "transformed," literally substituted, for someone or something else. Actual inorganic objects can be transformed into organic objects. For instance, suppose a play calls for the presence of a newborn baby in a scene. Naturally, a doll or some similar object, wrapped in blankets and swaddling clothes, will be substituted for the real object. But what do we usually see in the actor's supposedly real relationship to the baby? Seldom is the doll or bundle of rags made to "come to life" for the actor much less to the audience. Instead, he treats it closer to its real state; that of a doll or a dummy. The average actor will say that the audience will know it is only a doll, no matter how much he acts "real" in his relationship to it. This is not so! The audience is there to believe and it loves nothing so much as to become completely absorbed into whatever reality the skilled actor is able to create. If only every actor could realize how desperately the audience wants to believe and will believe if given the opportunity!

Even if he can arouse the slightest doubt in the minds of the audience as to whether or not the doll is a real infant, if he could just instill the possibility that it is a baby after all, the audience's involvement, their belief in other important scenes, and their belief in the stage relationships between the other actors will be greatly enhanced. Many scenes, indeed whole plays, have been considered either artistic successes or else written off completely depending upon the outcome of an actor's ability to extend himself in a logical piece of stage reality.

In the case of a doll wrapped in a blanket being "transformed" into a real baby, examine now how Substitutions are created imaginatively. They are really quite logical and are done with the utmost truth and simplicity. The acting student can use the exercise below for class work after practicing it in the privacy of his own room: As I stated previously, Substitution has Sense Memory as its natural foundation so it is with sensory objects that the actor must begin. The first thing he must determine, before using his senses, is a familiar mental picture of a real infant. His Sense Memory will begin with "seeing" the infant's features, eyes, face, nose, legs, toes, and fingers; as much of the child as he can recall in his mind's eye. This mental picture of the features, etc., must be substituted truthfully to himself as he looks at the doll. This is a relatively easy task. All he has to do as he relates to the doll is to *make the effort* to see the particulars of the real face of a baby in place of the doll's features. That is, actually try to remember sensorially each feature of the baby known *personally* to the actor and replace them in the doll.

Again, the emphasis is merely to make the effort and it will come. As his eyes try to meet those of the child, and as he establishes a *real* face with *real* features before him, the audience, too, will find its own recognition of the infant and will receive the impression that the actor is seeking to relate to a baby as a real person does in life. The audience will believe in the object and will realize that the actor is actually seeing something which to him is alive and real, not just an inanimate object.

The next step involves picking up the "baby" while continuing the inner mental work. How often we see actors handle stage properties in an unrealistic manner! When this happens the whole illusion of the object, in this case the "baby," is usually lost. Simplicity is important. When the actor slides his hands under the "baby" to pick it up, he must make the effort to determine the exact location of the baby's back, legs, arms, shoulders, and, most important, the neck and back of the head. For here is where firm support is needed by a helpless infant. He should make a sensory effort to establish the definite weight of a real baby for often the "prop" will be lighter, which, if not taken to mind, will cause the loss of some of the potential reality of the object.

As the actor progresses in his relationship to the object, he will automatically find himself trying to feel the outline through the blankets of the entire torso and legs as he cradles the infant in his arms with his sense of touch and sight. From this his imagination will also progress to where he will relate to the object just as one would in life. (He may hold the baby in a naturally subconscious way to detect a "wetting" or a whimper or perhaps speak to him, quite unlike the way he would had he not established the previous "realities.") The audience may see the actor recognize the baby's "smile," or his imperceptible attempts to communicate, all without the audience actually seeing the face of the baby but by this time willing to believe there is one on stage.

It is easy to see why good concentration is needed to carry out these tasks, as simple as they are, for the concentration is usually involved with several senses at once. The number of possibilities involved in such a seemingly simple exercise are many for the sense of sight, touch, perhaps sound, and even the sense of smell can be aroused. (It seems all babies have the odor of milk or baby powder about them.) The actor may find himself reaching down and taking hold of the little hand, or one of the fingers, making the effort to recall through Sense Memory exactly how a real baby's hand feels, how it grasps, how it wriggles. Much of the actor's own personality will come out of the task and to everything the actor does because the audience will be seeing not just an actor in a role but a live human being who relates in a very human and natural way. Also, a natural originality will be seen. This results because no one reacts in exactly the same way to an object; in this case an infant. If the tasks are carried out truthfully they will reflect the individual and *personal* qualities of the actor.

The sad state of lack of training on the actor's part is often seen in so obvious a situation as the one just described. Many actors do not realize that they must not restrict themselves to their own little sphere on stage. It is up to them to create the living quality needed from the "infant." They think acting ends for them with making themselves real when, in reality, that is exactly what they would really be doing if they would learn to relate truthfully to objects on stage.

Notice how easily small children adapt to this exercise. They have the innate gift of fantasy, turning a doll into a real baby, a mud pie structure into an unconquerable fortress. An actor can learn much from children. They are more honest. They are not frightened of the truth or of fantasy. And see how free their imaginations and sense of fantasy roam! This is a gift the actor should strive all his life to regain for it is nature's gift to us, one that we have pushed aside and cruelly neglected. A certain amount of fantasy can be invaluable to the artist for it allows his imagination to soar freely, gleaning from it impressionistic material to add to his store for future use.

Substitutions are used to great advantage with the articles found for stage use by the properties man. Swords, rifles, and glittering jewels, to name but a few, are invariably dummies, paste, or papier-mache. If these objects are not treated in a wholly realistic manner and made real to the actor, much of the realism of the actor's character, to say nothing of the veracity of the play and its plot, will be lost. To substitute the physical qualities of a stage property truthfully, as it might appear in life, is a service to the author second only to his written words.

It should now be easy to see how an actor might tie in a Substitution with a Personalization for if the object has a familiar or personal connotation to him it will be easier to substitute because of its personal qualities. An example of this would be the substitution of someone else's face, someone nearer and dearer to the actor than the actress playing opposite him in, say, a love scene. This may seem strange to the layman, but often the actor playing opposite another evokes none of the necessary qualities needed in the actor's stage relationships. When this situation arises a simple substitution of someone in the actor's own life, someone who may not even be like the character in the script, supplies the solution.

Sometimes the substitution will take on personal qualities and when it does, this is usually very good. Anything which makes an object closer, more familiar to the instrument and sense of understanding, should be used for the benefit of the role and the play in general.

Another instance arises when for some reason the actor cannot relate properly to the stage setting. If it is a room, he may not be able to relate his character to the room truthfully, the way the character would in life. This may happen quite often; especially in a low budget production where only a semblance of a room is all that is provided for actor and audience alike. The barrenness or cold atmosphere of strange surroundings may find no bond with the actor's instrument. In such a case, a substitution of an entire room, one familiar to the actor and which has the same meaning to him as the stage room has to the character he is portraying, can be accomplished with beautiful results. Again, this is done by merely substituting the interior of the room he has in mind for the one on stage complete to all items (furniture, draperies, rugs, the color of the walls, and bric-a-brac). As he does this, the stage furnishings will take on the aspect of complete reality, the reality of the actor's own furnishings. But what the audience will see is the character relating to a room that is his and is known best by him. Now the relationship between Personalization and Substitution is even stronger for the substituted room may take on very personal qualities and clearly lead into a Personalization. The results of this are unlimited, and qualities as yet unseen from the actor and his character, usually pour forth in that rare and welcome commodity known as originality.

Personalizations and Substitutions are as unchanged today as they were in Stanislavsky's day. They are used in modern Method teaching in this country. One exercise involving the use of these two important phases of the Method consists of taking an inanimate object such as an old pillow and treating it as a live object such as a small dog or cat. This is done by passing it around from student to student and letting each handle it as they would the real object in life. All of their imagination and sense of fantasy will come into play as they pass the "puppy" from one to another, being careful all the while to keep the "head" of the animal distinquished from the "tail" and bringing into focus the weight of the object being created, the touch, the color of the object, and so forth. This is just one exercise of many that can be improvised by student or teacher alike. This type of exercise that began with Stanislavsky passed on in use to his students, Vakhtangkov and M. Chekhov to name two, then on to Lee Strasberg, and on to Strasberg's students who now teach their own classes in acting. The objects in these exercises might be considered dear to us; a favorite puppy or an infant. Each student may display his own *personal* feelings about the object as he receives it when passed around and it will not be difficult to see what kind of relationship he has with the real object. This exercise, when done among a group of students, serves again to show to each student the close relation between Personalizations and Substitutions and how it is possible for the actor to utilize this relationship when the role calls for it.

In concluding this chapter, I think I ought to state two points. One, the work covered to this point has been mainly work of a mental kind though far from being theoretical, and the chapters with their exercises that follow will give the serious proponent of the Method an even clearer understanding of its practicability and purpose. And, two, in this chapter as well as every chapter the reader must realize that a state of completeness is not only impossible but perhaps undesirable, for the joy of art lies in its discovery for the individual. As the actor and his instrument grow together, one ever in search for awareness and truth, the other practicing and proving, the binding relationship among *all* phases of the Method will become open to view.

This is the height to which the modern actor should aspire; the fusing of all phases of his training into one highly effective instrument capable at will of producing simplicity, realism, clarity of image, and the unaffected spoken word.

Physical Exercises

Up to now, phases of the Method that stress mainly the mental work in acting have been discussed. In this chapter you will see how this mental work produces realistic results in creating *Physical Exercises*, sometimes called Character Exercises.

Young and old actors alike usually take great delight in training their instruments to respond to outward character "devices" that a play may demand such as regional speech traits, accents, and speech impediments or blindness, crippling effects such as limps deriving from an artificial leg, broken leg, or polio, to name but a few.

Authors, thankfully, invent many physical tasks for their characters but here a great danger lies. These tasks, unless done so realistically as to cause genuine interest and even concern in the audience, can and will be distracting by their lack of truth. Yes, actors love to get hold of a role that gives them some special activity to do with their bodies, one which presents a challenge of consistency and creativeness. Yet, very few are able to do them with realistic results. Fewer still are able to maintain the exercise consistently.

I include in this chapter several exercises which will lead the actor toward development of the ability to create any "character" activity that a play's role may require. In these exercises you will see the need to utilize much of what has already been discussed. Relaxation, Concentration, Sense Memory, Justification, and all the awareness learned from life will play important roles in the complete accomplishment of a Physical Exercise problem.

The complete understanding of the problem first of all is most important to its solution. An author may not tell the actor any more than that the character walks with a limp. (In this case, it would probably be a minor role, as larger roles would give a more detailed description.) It is then up to the actor to discover what kind of limp it is, what caused it, was he wounded in the war, was it an accident, a disease? When the answer is found it must be justified according to the play first, the actor second.

In other words, "Could the character have received his limp the way I have decided, in logical harmony with the tenets and interpretation of the author?"

This must be done without disrupting the unity of the play and blending in harmony with it. You may now ask why it is so important to know exactly what causes the character to walk the way he walks. What difference does it make how he walks so long as he limps? This is not so in life.

A person recovering from infantile paralysis will walk in a different manner than one who has been afflicted with rickets since childhood. A person with a prosthesis will walk differently from someone with a clubfoot. If these differences are justified to the actor himself, they will in turn justify the lines spoken to another actor in the play. This relationship that evolves from the Physical Exercise, coupled with the plot and lines of the play, will then be justified to the audience. The audience must never be placed in permanent doubt as to the nature of a Physical Exercise unless this has been specified by the author. They must know what has gone before so that your actions and the author's lines will be justified to them in accordance with the "accident" or "deformity." The Physical Exercise must be clearly defined as it would be in life.

When we meet someone in life who has been unfortunate enough to have had a disease or accident that has left him disabled, we may not query him as to its nature. We usually let him volunteer any information concerning it even though we may become well acquainted. But this is not to say we are indifferent to it, that we do not wonder, and finally decide to our own satisfaction what the origin of the disablement is, even before he discusses it. To do this is human nature and it is only when we cannot reach such a decision that we will sometimes discreetly ask for ourselves. This is why in life we understand more clearly some of a person's actions and words when we find out he has suffered a tragic experience. These actions and words probably were produced as a result of the experience which, hitherto, might have been misunderstood. On the other hand, the audience is unable to ask either the actor or the author. This is why they must not be left in the dark. The actor's motivations must be clearly drawn so as to justify his every line and to give his Physical Exercise the consistency of life on stage.

The first exercise you attempt does not necessarily have to be the one that follows. It can be one of your own choosing, particularly so if there is an easier one for you than the one I have chosen. These exercises are especially useful for classroom work with a competently trained teacher supplying the criticism.

The problem in the following exercise involves that of a character who has a *curvature of the spine*. Do not try to make the character older or younger than you are. It is a natural tendency to do this as a curvature seems to project advanced age in most people's minds. Let your "character" be your age. Let him be *you* with a curvature.

EXERCISE I

(A) Sit in a straight-back chair and make the effort to relax. Close your eyes and for a few minutes of preparation try to get your body in a position whereby you could fall asleep if need be.
(B) As you begin the exercise, try to find exactly where the curve in the spine begins and where it ends. Is the lower half of the back straight, the curve beginning midway up to the top of the shoulders? (This will depend on the individual

actor's decision and the extent to which he wishes to develop the exercise.)

(C) Rise from the chair and take a few steps keeping the body relaxed. Keep the concentration on the area of the back, particularly the spine.

(D) Try to find through Sense Memory which muscles would be affected by such an affliction. Then make the effort to relax them.

(E) Walk around the stage a little more. Try to become aware of how the curve would affect your balance. Does it throw you forward when you walk? Would such an affliction affect any other parts of your body? Would it make your arms hang differently? Would it cause a strain on other muscles in the back or shoulders, thereby making them stronger and more powerful, or would it weaken them?

(F) Notice now the attitude of the neck. Would the curve affect the neck? If the neck is affected, the carriage of the head will be too.

(G) Is the head affected so that the face is made to look downward more so than is normal.

(H) Maintain that part of the exercise you have discovered is true for you while walking as *naturally* as you can with it.

NOTE: It is important for the actor to realize that a person with a curvature of the spine *does not try to walk like a person with a curvature of the spine*. He tries to walk like a normal, healthy person. The same is true of anyone with an affliction. The effort is *to be like everyone else, to be normal*. Therefore, the attempt is always to walk as erect as you possibly can *behind* the affliction, always making the effort to hold the head up, in the case of the curvature in a normal position. Actually as we know from life, this usually only serves to accentuate the affliction more so.

This exercise should be done many times; each time adding another daily operation such as tying your shoes, drying the dishes, or getting dressed. Each time you do it you should find something new about your "character" and become aware of any differences you may note.

The problem in Exercise I is that of a curvature of the spine and, of course, it is impossible to actually curve the spine. But then how often do we actually see the curve on a fully clothed person? What the actor must do is create the feeling of the curve to himself, thereby giving the impression of it to the audience. It is only when the actor can live the exercise through, creating to himself by whatever means he can the clear manifest feelings of the exercise, will he accomplish the reality in it.

Just as a cripple does not try to walk like a cripple, an aged person does not try to walk as if he were old. The reality of the situation is that he *is* crippled or that he *is* old. Even a blind man tries to see, not with his eyes, but with every part of his body. He utilizes all his other senses to "see" for him by means of feeling, hearing, or smelling. A mute tries to "hear" by reading lips or by learning dactylology. These are the truths of life and an actor must find these any way he can. He must examine microscopically the reasons for certain afflictions. How does someone with one leg manage to walk with a prosthetic device? Where is the shift in balance with the artificial limb? What is it like to see over long periods of time with one eye? What causes rickets and how does it affect the functions of the legs? What would it be like to be unable to see at all? Or walk at all? Often a study of the disease is helpful in finding the clue or the answer to a problem.

One afternoon I saw Lee Strasberg walking out of a subway station as I was entering. He didn't see me. He was engrossed in watching a blind man make his way unaided toward the trains. The man did not have a seeing-eye dog, only a cane, but he went straight to the right platform and boarded *his* train, after letting one pass, without asking any directions from anybody. Lee turned around and boarded the same train, which immediately sped off somewhere in the direction of Brooklyn. I could see him through the windows of the train as it left, with a quizzical furrowed brow, the beady eyes staring through thick glasses, intently observing his quarry. The funny thing was that I could not help wondering how many times he had done this before.

Everyone familiar with George Bernard Shaw's *Saint Joan*

will remember that the role of the Dauphin of France is that of a man wholly lacking in the courage of his convictions. He is weak though well-meaning, but full of the fears that do not usually characterize the strength needed for a future leader of a nation. He loves France but fears her people; he loves Joan and, yet, fears what the rejection of her will mean in the eyes of God; he fears the British but also respects them. He is filled with nearly every kind of emotional insecurity. On top of all this, he is said to be of a questionable blood line which gives rise to doubt about his legitimacy and therefore to his right to succession to the throne. Even the populace of France speaks of it openly. Because he is sensitive to his own shortcomings and ineffectualness, he is prone to give vent to outbursts that sometimes makes him seem quite mad. Actually, he wants only to please but, by his weakness, is unable to cope with anything and only succeeds in hastening Joan's death and the moral destruction of France.

To create all the facets of a character like the Dauphin would seem a formidable challenge for any actor. The casting of Siobhan McKenna for the title role in the New York production at the Phoenix Theatre was excellent, but the casting of Michael Wager in the role of the Dauphin was brilliant.

Wager's characterization depicted all the frailties of human nature which the Dauphin possessed while, at the same time, preserving the strength that even the weakest person will display when pushed too far. He was pitiful but somehow comic; submissive yet dynamic in his passiveness. He could be erudite and at other times only childish; at still other times, he seemed almost insane. On stage, Wager presented all the facets of a living, breathing human being caught up in circumstances that were beyond his all too human limitations.

I was powerfully impressed with his interpretation having seen several productions of the play previously but none done with the amount of insight shown here with the role of the Dauphin. It did not take long to discover how he accomplished what he did.

A stickler with regard to historical realities, Wager cut his own hair to the style of the time of the play, the fifteenth century. For anyone not familiar with this type of haircut, it can be best duplicated by placing a small bowl on top of the head and then shaving several inches above the top of the ears around the entire head and as close to the scalp as possible. The effect was startlingly authentic. But this only aided, not created, the outer emotional feeling for weakness that he desired for his role. To do this, Wager chose a simple but very effective Physical Exercise that touched the trigger to the very heart of his characterization.

During rehearsals he took his script and circled in red every one of his lines that began with the letter B. Every line was spoken normally until he reached a word beginning with this letter. Then he would hopelessly stammer, barely managing to get the word out of his mouth. As soon as he was able to say the word, he would proceed unhesitatingly with the rest of his lines until he reached another word beginning with B. The effect was humorously grotesque, as fits the character, and lent just the correct sense of weakness needed in his role. Needless to say, this one simple Physical Exercise was done consistently and well; so well that several members of the audience commented on the cleverness of hiring an actor who stuttered. The significance of his choice of a Physical Exercise, however, is made apparent with our ever-increasing knowledge of psychology, for the manifestations of a stutterer lend a great deal of insight into the background of the character. Stuttering is not a speech defect! Stuttering is a nervous condition that is imposed on children usually by overanxious parents. I am sure that even in the fifteenth century this fact was realized innately by a stutterer just as it is today though they are not familiar with the psychological nature of their affliction.

I propose you follow Exercise II or one of your own choosing that is similar. You should not necessarily attempt an exercise simply because it is in this book. Simpler exercises of your own choosing can be done first to ascertain if the instrument is working fully and in the right direction. The primary purpose of the exercises in this book is to act as a *guide* in doing any exercises contained in each chapter. The actor must also realize that the exercises are not necessarily complete with regard to the questions he can ask himself. The questions I have included are guides to an infinity of questions that are possible to ask oneself. Each individual should find new questions, therefore new facets of his work, with each attempt at the exercises.

Let us now proceed with Exercise II which concerns *walking with a prosthetic device (an artificial leg)*. There will be a number of technical problems which the actor will have to find out for himself. These have to be solved before he can effectively accomplish the exercise.

For instance, he will have to know the manner in which such devices are attached to the rest of the body, the materials from which they are made (steel, wood, plastic, leather), how much they weigh, and how a person learns to walk with them (balance, shift of weight, stride, maneuverability). Also, the real leg will have to "become" the artificial one. It must respond to you like an artificial leg, not like your own leg. When these questions and any others pertinent to the exercise are answered, he is ready to begin.

EXERCISE II

(A) Make the preparations regarding relaxation as in Exercise I and previous exercises. Take as long as you feel you need. Four or five minutes for relaxation is not considered too long for this exercise as the body needs to be completely relaxed mentally and physically in order to keep the concentration on the tasks.

(B) As you sit in the chair, make the effort to feel the exact locations of the attachments of the artificial limb. This can be done through Sense Memory and if you are unable to "feel" all of them, do not worry. You can return to this phase later in this exercise.

- NOTE: It is important for the actor to realize that this is strictly an exercise in finding realities and should not be done in a "performing" manner, either in class or even for himself.

(C) Shift the body slightly and feel the weight of the limb. It is best at this point for you to use the actual weight of your own limb for the artificial one.

(D) Try to feel how the dead weight of the limb serves as an anchor when the body tries to move away from it.

(E) Rise from the chair slowly (not as one accustomed to using such a limb) so as to let the Sense Memory function on every development involving motion.

(F) Take a step or two, keeping the concentration on the tasks you have set for yourself. These tasks can be kept to a minimum at the first attempt at the exercise but should include basically all the Sense Memory aspects in the order that they occur. For example, the sense of the straps and paraphernalia that attach themselves to specific parts of the body, the weight of your own leg without using the leg muscles to move it and, also, the sense of touch as the foot is placed on the floor. Obviously the foot of an artificial leg has no feeling and, yet, the person wearing one will know it is touching the floor. Where will *he* feel it?

(G) Take several more steps very slowly and discover for yourself that the dead weight of the leg is actually moved by the rest of the body. Learn *how* this is done yourself by slowly turning and shifting the body in a manner that will move the leg in a forward position.

(H) After doing this for a few minutes, try to move the leg so that it will carry you backwards; then try it so you can move sideways.

After this exercise is practiced to the point where it shows progress in developing the sensory aspects of it, the actor should experiment further, always making sure that the movements are "justified" with regard to Sense Memory. After still further practice the actor should act a short scene for class and try to maintain the exercise while still retaining the main line of the play.

Remember that it is very easy to have your Physical Exercise convert your character into a caricature instead of a being that truly lives on stage. For this reason the actor must use restraint in all of the exercises, especially when applied to actual scene or stage work. They must be done with a subtlety found only in life. Do not try to do them with indicative movements and gesture but, instead, do them only as the realities are created to the individual. In this way each movement, each line of the play, will be incorporated and will fully complement the other. In this way the actor's full justification will be achieved by these realities. Furthermore, if one sense is not achieved at the desired time, don't be afraid to go back and try to capture it. You can do this easily enough even with advanced exercises being done in a play. Many times a certain sense will not come immediately but the actor must go on to the next task at hand. When one sense is working well, go back a little and explore with concentration the one which was omitted. It will usually appear in full strength when attempted now.

Throughout these exercises the actor must make a conscious effort to deal with any tension that may arise. If in the middle of the exercise he becomes aware that he is not relaxed in a certain part of his body, he should divert his concentration to that area and remove the tension. After all, in life wouldn't a person in the same circumstances try to relieve any pressure, tension, or nervous disturbance that is present?

Other Physical Exercises will contain more sensory objects to be worked on such as a broken arm or leg. In addition to the presense of the cast, splints, etc., there may well be an element of pain.

Later on in the development of the work you will see how the text of a play which makes note of, say, a person with a broken leg, touches the preparatory work done on the exercise. You may now see how closely Affective Memory can tie in with this work.

Animal Exercises

In acting, as in all arts, there comes a time when one may find an indefinable obstruction that seems to prevent parts of his instrument from functioning the way they should. These obstructions or mental blocks are often of an intangible nature. Yet, their destructive influence is anything but intangible. The creative processes (imagination and awareness) are most sorely affected. When this occurs we feel that something is missing in ourselves, something prevents us from grasping an integral part of the character we are portraying. We know it is missing but are unable to find it. What is worse is that we do not know how to go about finding it, putting our finger on the one element that could possibly tie all the aspects of a role together.

When this negative influence strikes we seem helpless to do anything about it. The most essential portions of the actor's instrument (imagination and deep insight) seem to be stilted and superficial in their activity.

The following work does not attempt to be a cure-all for this problem but will, I believe, lend a helping hand to many problems of character portrayal. The actor will see that a thorough appreciation and understanding of Animal Exercises will be of special service to his development and training as an actor-artist. Also, as we approach the two succeeding chapters on character creation, it is hoped that they will assist immeasurably in making use of all previous

144

work discussed so as to be included in the work on Outer Character and Inner Character.

The phase of the Method discussed in this chapter has long been a favorite of Lee Strasberg's students. Strasberg learned of these exercises from one of his former teachers, Madame Maria Ouspenskaya, who brought them intact to this country from her native Russia. In one of the many splinter groups of acting teachers that came originally to Stanislavsky to study and learn from the Master, eventually leaving and forming their own schools and theatres, was Vakhtangov for one and Ouspenskaya for another. The Animal Exercises Ouspenskaya stressed so strongly have gained a popularity and recognition in the Western theatre that is unmatched in Russia. The reasons for this are negligible; however, the importance of the exercises today cannot be denied. Strasberg maintains the exercises as a standard part of the student's work in his classes, placing a high degree of importance on them as do all serious proponents of Stanislavsky's system.

This phase of the Method known as Animal Exercises is actually a limitless number of acting exercises in animal characterization. The purposes of the exercises are twofold: (1) To assist the actor in a more complete understanding of his fellow man in order to portray him more truthfully on the stage, and (2) To use the animal characterizations, partially or even totally, in an actual role.

It is true, we say, that actors *should* be able to learn everything concerning human behavior from their associations and observations of other human beings around them. They *should* be able to study human habits, demeanor, characteristics, and thinking processes with an insight capable of capturing completely the essence of any role. Unfortunately, such is rarely the case for in actuality only the most superficial and evident details are usually grasped, leaving out the inherent differences present in every human being. Moreover, we tend to lack imagination in contrasting and distinguishing these differences. Consequently, we see everyone as being basically the same. Nothing could be further from the truth and even though objectively we know that every person is different, in the study of other people actors always seem to lean toward subjectivity. When this happens, insight, keen observation, and even concentration are destroyed.

No one knows for certain why it is so difficult to disassociate ourselves from our fellows thereby missing basic, important knowledge about ourselves when beginning a characterization for a role. The reasons for this vary with each individual. But, without trepidation of dispute, the fact remains that the human being is also an animal of only superior intelligence and can therefore learn much from the study of other animals. For these reasons we turn to the exercises in this chapter.

To begin with, the work is divided into two parts: (1) *Preparatory* and (2) *The Exercises Themselves*. In the first part we find, happily, that our observation tends to become quite objective for a change and our imagination seems to know no bounds. This results from a detailed study of the animal you have chosen to study for your exercise and it is in itself an interesting and rewarding part of the work.

As proof of the undivided attention we are able to give to animals, I offer the crowds of people standing outside the cage of an animal in a zoo. Watch them become absorbed in the antics of a monkey. At times they will even take on the innate dimensions of the beast itself. The onlooker will jiggle, move and react, curl his lips, chatter, and even scratch himself as the beast does. Of course, this may be done jokingly, if not unconsciously, but serves to point out how we tend to lose most of our inhibitions in their presence. Certainly we would not let ourselves imitate another human being so loosely and defiantly in public. For that matter, let a monkey or a chimpanzee come on stage in a play and see what happens. The actors will almost fade into the background as all attention is riveted on the animal because the naturalness of the animal's actions are more enjoyable to the audience than what they had hitherto been watching. Ask any seasoned actor if he enjoys acting with an animal on stage, or even a baby for that matter. Because they have not been rehearsed and because their actions are unrestrained and completely natural, we give animals more of our attention, understanding, and even our sympathy than we do our fellow man on stage or in life.

This first Preparatory work, that is, the *study* of the animal which leads to the exercises themselves, has been found to possess all the qualities which permit a heightened awareness to function. The work stimulates imaginative processes so necessary to the actor's art. The study of a specific animal must first begin with the actor's observation. This observation must be a most detailed kind and must assimilate the animal's peculiarities liberally, item by item. Since actors are by and large city people, the best place to observe animals is in the zoo.

For the first study, it will probably be best for the actor to choose a primate which possesses some qualities easily identifiable with man. This would, of course, include any of the monkey or ape groups such as chimpanzees and gorillas. However, if the actor has a familiar household pet, either dog or cat, it will be expedient to use it for study because of its convenience and because of the intimacy with the animal. One very important aspect to remember is that a thorough comprehensive study can rarely be made in one afternoon. Animals have many peculiarities, moods, and traits that appear at varied times. You will notice these changes with each visit to the zoo and learn to recognize, quite literally, what particular ''state of mind'' your animal is in that particular day. You may find him to be active and playful one day and sullen, or even belligerent the next, just as happens with human beings.

For clarification, we shall use the gorilla for a hypothetical study in this chapter. The first observations of the gorilla should include the physical manifestations prevalent in his every action. These will consist of the animal's manner of moving about his cage, the way he sits, how he eats, how he watches objects around him, which things attract his attention more than others, and very important, too, the animal's concentration on them. You will find quite early in your animal study that some animals seem to possess a phenomenal sense of concentration. This will be obvious to you when you see something which is of interest to the animal.

From these outward actions of the animal you must then begin studying their causes; that is, the inner impulses that motivate *actions*. In other words, why does he lumber along the way he does, why does he turn his head in a certain manner, why does he eat a certain way? You will notice a certain dexterity with his fingers that other animals do not have. Notice his bulk, how the power, weight, and strength are centered mostly in the upper back, neck, chest, and shoulders, hence the forward tilt to his gait with the knuckles and hands serving as a means of balance. Notice, too, that while the gorilla's legs are not weak, for they do serve to propel and to carry a proportion of his tremendous bulk, they certainly are not the strongest part of his body as is true in the human being. The beast has speed and agility when necessary. This seems to come from a driving rear end that propels him much the same way as the little three-wheeled cars. He moves, as he sits, in a completely relaxed manner using a minimum expenditure of energy. The ape is most interesting to us when he is engrossed in some simple operation such as playing with a toy, eating a meal, or romping with another ape. It is then that we see the rapt concentration in his eyes, the sure deftness in his fingers as he peels a banana, or inspects a rag doll. The eye movements of a gorilla are so nearly human in their seeing as to keep the observer absorbed in their direction and object of attention. However, as human as their eyes seem, they possess a quality rarely constant in human eyes: A complete mirrorization of the beast's real thoughts. This is why they hold our attention. We believe ourselves to be able to tell practically what he is thinking. There are no inhibitory factors with him and his thoughts and emotions do not hide in his eyes but, instead, reflect clearly what lies behind them.

When discovering the motivations which drive the animal externally, the actor must then analyze them carefully. He must take into consideration other factors: The animals' present surroundings, the cages which hold them and their relationship to it; what it means, if anything, to gorillas to be caged. This part of the study can be most stimulating to the actor's imagination and helps him to perceive what differences would exist if the beast were now in his natural habitat.

The actor next distinguishes the basic differences between the animal's body and his own. For the purpose of doing the exercise, he should begin to think in terms of making his body function and react like that of the animal he is studying. There will be many observations to make; more than this chapter could hold, and it is important for the actor to discover them himself.

When beginning the exercises he will find that his will and concentration play important roles in the exercise as do his imagination and relaxation. In particular, relaxation must be constantly striven for in these exercises. Along with a strong will, concentration, actors' imagination, and relaxation, there will also be the need somewhere in the study to grasp the elements which most typify the animal you are characterizing. Some of these I have previously mentioned, but there will be more, many more, as you will see. This is why a detailed study of the animal is so necessary. If these elements are not grasped, understood, and carefully thought out truthfully, it would be impossible to create them in a role with the subtlety and elusive delicacy that is usually demanded of them.

For those readers not familiar with the role of Willy Loman in Arthur Miller's *Death of A Salesman*, I can best describe the role that incorporates a physical image of tremendous burdens into the character; an oppressive weight brought about by guilt and failure. Lee J. Cobb originated the role on Broadway and his lucid interpretation was nothing less than genius inspired. Cobb was a relatively young man when he played this role of a man in his sixties, he could not rely on his natural age in the character portrayal of Willy. It is said that he first experimented with weights tied to his legs, back, and shoulders in order to acquire the feeling of an old man carrying the troubles of a lifetime for the whole world to see. If this story is true, I am sure he found it quite impractical and, possibly, beneath his art. For in his finished interpretation he possessed all the needed qualities of the character to the fullest degree and they are created by his own artistry, not with mechanical contrivances. It is generally known among theatre people that he had used an Animal Exercise throughout each performance to achieve the desired effect. It wasn't hard to guess which animal because the lumbering, yet surefooted, and sometimes stoic nature of the character could only have come from the patient, long-suffering elephant.

Cobb's Willy Loman contained the sheer bulk which comes from being overweight, which Cobb isn't, and the feeling of the miseries in Loman's life that inexorably kept beating and battering him down. He captured the one essence of the animal that suggests heaviness in nearly everything he does while still being nimble enough to escape the gloom prevailing in the final blow of his life. He spent many an hour of study with persevering insight to create the sensitive, all too human portrait of Willy Loman. I mention the case of Lee J. Cobb's characterization strictly as an example of how a Physical Exercise is actually used in the characterization of one of the greatest performances ever seen on the New York stage.

The actual performance of the Animal Exercises should be done first under supervision in a classroom using either an imaginary surrounding or the reality of the stage itself. In the former, sensory objects such as the bars of a cage can accompany the exercise. Whereas, if the reality of the stage is used, everything on it can be utilized in relation to the way the animal would react to them. This latter method is sometimes better for the first attempt at the exercise just because it does not have additional concentration and sensory objects to include in the work. Keeping the exercise simple and uncluttered in your first attempts may prove to be more rewarding in the end for all the actor's concentration must be summoned and put to the test in these exercises.

It would be impossible for me to draw a specific chart of how to follow an Animal Exercise from beginning to end, or to tell the actor what to add, or which to eliminate in the exercise without first seeing the exercise done. Much will depend on the individual's instrument and its adaptability to the work. I can, however, include an outline that will give the reader a more than general idea of what premises to work from in the exercises. From then on in class he must depend on the insight of his teacher who will guide the individual's instrument in the proper direction.

OUTLINE FOR ANIMAL EXERCISE—GORILLA

I. It is best to begin the exercise in the same attitude as done in all the earlier chapters. Sit in a chair and work first for complete physical and mental relaxation. When you feel this essential beginning has been achieved, the concentration can then be transferred to the tasks already chosen.

II. Animal Exercises usually are more readily accomplished by a reverse technique, hitherto frowned upon in the earlier work discussed in this book. That is, an outward approach leading to the inner life of the animal instead of the inner impulses fomenting the outer manifestations and characteristics that produce the desired result.

In the exercise it is best to begin with a sheer physical presentation of the animal as derived from the observation-study. The physical attitude such as the animal "posture," stance, body, arm and head movements should begin purely technically, using the concentration to guide the body in adapting to the "transformation." The power of the actor's will is usually called on at this stage of the exercise more so than in any of the previous work covered.

III. Accompanying this purely outward technique must be the logic for his physical actions; why he moves the way he does, and why his body adapts itself to its particular positions for movement. This will be afforded by the aforethought of the observations and study of the animal's physical structure designed for these positions and, also, his animal-like motivations; weight, location of power and strength in his body, and, most important, his balance.

IV. While the outer physical appearance and manner of the animal is being worked on, the actor must then begin to work for the inner life of the animal. He will find that he can utilize his own human intelligence, concentration, insight, and sensitivity to achieve the subintelligence prevalent in the beast. Animals do not possess high reasoning faculties as do humans, but, instead, behave by a conditioned and sometimes innate instinct.

V. Whereas, we have always believed realities to be of a constant, stable nature representing the unswerving truth of existence and of situations, we now discover that in the case of Animal Exercises there are many objects possessing one seemingly truthful reality at first glance, but which in actuality has a totally different reality to the animal; one that is equally veracious but as diverse as imaginable. For instance, when an animal sees an object like a coat, he does not see it as a human sees it. He does not "see" the style, the cut, fit, length, warmth, or any of the other human aspects of it. The beast may, instead, inspect it as to the feel of the cloth, the smell, or the taste. He may treat it as a plaything, or even a possible danger; almost any way except the purpose for which it was intended. To the beast the reality of objects, and even situations, are on an entirely different level but are as real to them as they are to us. Only if a relatively superior primate such as a gorilla or a chimpanzee were to observe someone putting on or removing a coat, would he then maybe attempt to duplicate the act. But even this would no doubt be done for his own amusement or for an entirely different reason than that of his human counterpart.

The actor now realizes that if the animal were on the stage in acting class, he would not see the stage in the same reality as the actor (as a place where scenes are presented, where creativity is produced). Neither would he see objects such as tables, chairs, lamps, silverware, or clothing in the same reality as the actor. This would hold true anywhere in the animal's environment and existence. These articles would all be seen in a different, if not indifferent, light to the animal.

Conversely, the human and social connotations of the jungle bush hold one reality for us but a completely different one for the gorilla. Therefore, the actor's concentration must be centered, to a degree, on staying away from, actually refraining from all human recognition to, objects, sounds, or sensory "human realities" which exist in the classroom while he is doing the exercise.

VI. If he looks out into the classroom just in time to see a student entering the room, he tries to see a form in its entirety (one not separated as to articles of clothing and body, not as "Mary Johnson the actress," a talent, a personality). He sees, instead, something that can be rationalized only so far as his limited intelligence can absorb. This rationalization can be augmented only by the facilities provided by nature and includes every sensory ability provided him. To explain this moving form he cannot use reason. He must rely upon his sense of smell, hearing, and whatever else to explain the "form" he has seen. If "Mary Johnson" speaks, the animal would not be able to relate to word meanings as we know them. He would, instead, try to relate to the sounds as pitch, tone, volume, or even inflection to determine whether or not the "form" is something that holds a relationship to "reality" to him. Is the "form" something that will bring his food? Or is it a potential danger? He would not recognize the styling of her high-heeled shoes or even be aware that they have a separate existence from the "form" itself, unless demonstrated by removing them in his presence.

The ape may express an interest in the clacking *sound* of heels against the floor, first determining where the sound originated and then listening, watching, sniffing. In short, he uses all the senses at his command to try to relate the sounds to his limited comprehension. Only then would he possibly show a concentrated interest in the shoes.

VII. After the characterization of the animal has been attained, the teacher can test the student's power of concentration, imagination, and improvisation by doing some little task designed to draw the "animal's" attention. A shuffling of his feet, whistling, or swinging a watch fob can serve to ascertain how deeply concentrated the actor is in the exercise by then observing his reactions to the task. The "animal," and by this time I mean the actor characterizing the animal, may be interested in any sudden movement, noise, or swirl of clothing that may seem novel or may present a potential threat to him. This interest will be stimulated by the depth of the actor's concentration in *being* the animal. For even while his concentration and sense of the animal is employed, the actor still retains his human sensibilities which he uses to make any improvisational adjustments.

The above is the line of thinking the actor must maintain while doing the exercises. All of the knowledge attained from the preparatory work, from the reasons for the animal's walk to his absorbing curiosity, can be realized by the actor's instrument. It might be good for actors to regain some of the innate qualities prevalent in all animals which have been lost, to a great extent, by us over centuries of civilization. More of the simple, honest curiosity with regard to our art might be a healthy beginning, too. The honesty supplied by nature should be our teacher for she alone is constant in realism and only with reality can acting be considered a truly creative art.

Before closing this chapter, let me impress again upon those readers who may tend to overlook or even underestimate Animal Exercises that (even though they may seem strange to some) their importance is great in the actor's training. It is true that they may seem strange to some at first, especially to an actor not familiar with them but who tries to imagine himself doing them, whereas the average reader probably would not see anything strange in the exercises since actors are always doing crazy things anyway.

The exercises I have outlined may lead the reader to believe that they are easy to do and can therefore be skipped over in the actor's training. Let me assure the reader that while the Method varies in its acceptance and facility with each individual, the work as a whole tends to demand a great portion of the actor's implementation. This is not to imply that all facets of the Method can never be absorbed by one individual and put to practical use. They can and have been many times over. One facet of the Method often depends upon another for its thorough understanding and application. For this reason, none of the important groupings as listed, outlined, and discussed in this book should be eliminated.

Let me suggest that the reader who thinks Animal Exercises are too easy for him attempt a *simple* Animal Exercise: characterizing a pigeon. If he can carry this exercise through completely for his teacher, it is conceded that his instrument is far enough advanced to warrant his progressing to other phases of the work. This is not to say, however, that he should not periodically return to *Animal Exercises* to keep his instrument in practice.

I think it only fair to inform the reader that characterizing a pigeon is usually considered to be the most difficult of all Animal Exercises. The coordination between the head and the rest of the body is completely foreign to all other animals.

Creating the
Inner Character

The components of Stanislavsky's system, as I have covered them in the preceding chapters, must be utilized whenever it is necessary to create what is called the Inner Character of the role. My purpose in grouping these components is possibly a subjective one due to my own experience in learning and teaching the Method, and it is not necessarily a set pattern of study or a panacea recommended for everyone. With one exception, any of the phases of the Method can be studied separately or collectively in a dramatics class. Some may even be learned and practiced and then applied to actual stage work right in the privacy of your own room provided a thorough understanding and awareness of existing problems are present. It is certainly possible and often quite desirable for the exercises in Chapter Twelve to be done before those in Chapter Eleven. Work including all the phases can also be done simultaneously.

However, I will say again that the Sense Memory work covered in Chapter Three *must* precede any of the work that follows. It must be continually worked on throughout the actor's life because Sense Memory is the base on which the greatest part of the work depends. Only when the senses are trained to remember on stage, as they do in life, can the subsequent work be done with a complete command of realism. When the phases of modern Method, as set forth in this book, are understood and are subjected to fulfillment by the actor's instrument, he then possesses a repertoire of pure technique with which to call on for the creation of Inner Character.

There are many actors who have not been trained in the manner of which I have written, Judith Anderson and Charles McCawley, to name but two—and yet, they always manage to possess and project the inner sensitivity of a role, encompassing the necessary essence of it to create a profound and rich performance. Perhaps they are not constant in outstandingly striking performances and possibly this is where any fault lies with regard to their own artistic fulfillment.

Then there is the mistaken school of thought comprised of all too many writers and teachers of dramatics who proclaim that there are "personalities" like Katherine Cornell, Tallulah Bankhead, or Helen Hayes who only have to stand in front of an audience to satisfy them, more so than an actor who transforms himself for his role completely. These same authors of acting textbooks claim that some actors possess a "stage presence, radiance, and inherent vitality" that is reward enough to the beholder, and that to try to separate their personalities from their roles would be a great loss. I say that the loss of such people as these, who are in a position to profess such idiotic notions to the impressionable young of the theatre, would be a great step forward in promoting a healthier theatre in America and the rest of the Western world. This school of thought is very dangerous to art.

How do these people think such actors achieved their "radiant personalities" in the first place if it were not for having earned them even if at the beginning of their careers? No artist should be content to stand on past fame. If an actor is to retain the loyalty of the public as well as that of his fellow artists, his quest for knowledge of his craft, his love of life, his sensitivity, and never-ending search for reality must remain with him always.

It was and is the pure artistic creativity of actors such as Tommaso Salvini, Eleanora Duse, Laurette Taylor, John Geilgud, Paul Muni, Edmund Kean, and the Booths, plus all too few more, that has enabled the theatre in the Western world to achieve the heights it has reached. I am equally certain that the ''personalities'' referred to in this naive school of thought would be the first to disagree with it and to admit in the consciences of their innermost selves that their successes were based not on any magical powers or individuality long past but, instead, on hard work derived from artistic desire and creative fulfillment. They would be able to point to their financial as well as artistic flops as proof of their personal vulnerability to audiences because they have all had them.

As he approaches the problems and tasks concerned with finding the Inner Character, the actor can begin by a simple and direct character analysis using the awareness of his own instrument to accumulate information about the character which must then be regarded as fact. I say fact because this information must be gathered objectively in much the same light as a statistician or census-taker would gather them. The actor's own relationship to the Inner Character he is portraying must be subjective only in *how* he will play the knowledge he has found, not *what* he will play as the character.

The actor's awareness of what is needed for the creation of Inner Character can be greatly stimulated by asking himself honestly, as the character, a series of questions pertinent to the life of the character. In the final analysis of the character, he must arrive at logical and concrete answers. For example: Who am I? What are my particular likes and dislikes? Do I have a hobby? Am I religious? Which religion do I believe in? What is my background? What did my father do for a living? What was my day like? On what street do I live? (Be able to describe the street.) What does my apartment look like? How many rooms do I have? (Give a full description of the type of living quarters that you as the character might inhabit. Give particular detail to the furnishings.) What did I do today? Who did I talk to? What is my basic relationship to the other characters in the play? What is my political outlook or my views on the world situation at the time of this play?

This is to name but a few of the myriad questions possible to ask oneself as the character. When the actor begins to "live" the life of his character, as will be demonstrated by the truthfulness of the answers he gives to his self-imposed questions, he can then create the situations that spring from the author's words by applying the technique he has accumulated in his training.

He must learn to work on what the character thinks, feels, and believes, his personal habits and possible traits just as if he actually lived. He must remember that inner feelings are created by real emotion and not by the eye; whatever distracts the audience's attention from the scene is fatal. Therefore, the actor's movements, including gesticulations, must be governed by the inner life he creates and not by conventional dictates. He must not forget the wonderful possibilities to be gleaned from an appreciation of the other creative arts. He can observe paintings which depict the outer life of a character such as his but will also sometimes present a vivid clue to his inner spirit. The actor can ask himself what type of music a character such as this would enjoy. He can then listen at length to pieces of this music, deciding which passages the character would like best and, more important, why.

As the actor's understanding of the Inner Character becomes sharp and clear, he will find that his instrument is more readily able to respond to the tasks at hand. With a full character analysis will come relaxation, an easy response of the senses, and concentration.

There is now, with more television and movies being produced than ever before, a feeling among young actors and actresses that unless their role is a major one it is unnecessary to put forth all of one's effort and capabilities. These young people tend to become lazy and are often content to satisfy no more than just the outward direction supplied by the script. As a result they work outwardly and superficially and serve no artistic purpose in the play. This is particularly true in the United States, whereas in Britain there is a somewhat healthier attitude, not akin to the "star" complexes so prevalent in this country.

For instance, in England where repertory theatre flourishes it is not strange to see three leading actors on the same bill in a play with only one leading role. The remaining two will play a supporting role and maybe even a bit part. Several weeks later, however, you will see a changing of the parts with last month's leading actor playing a supporting minor role. And how challenging, how full those minor roles can be played! We in this great country of ours should strive just a little more for dedication to the theatre and a lot less to ourselves. For no matter how small an actor's role may be, he should enter into it with the same enthusiasm for truth as he would a larger role.

But you may ask how a part that is hardly more than a walk-on with no specific description or purpose of his part given by the author, except to fill a street or crowd scene, can be made to come alive with a singular expressiveness and veracity. Years ago, at the beginning of my studies with Lee Strasberg, a good example was shown us of the extent to which an actor can go to create his Inner Character. Rare though this case is, it points up the laudable sincerity that some actors have regarding their art.

An actor friend of Strasberg's was given a job as an extra in a play. He was in only one scene in the whole play and it was to have taken place in a tavern. His was the opening scene that had the two leading actors sitting at a table unfolding the plot to the audience while he was to sit calmly supplying nothing more than his physical presence to the scene as a "customer" at the bar.

The two actors playing the leading roles were well-suited for their parts and enjoyed considerable reputation for their acting abilities. At the end of an early rehearsal of the scene everyone watching it agreed that the two leads were very good, their parts thoroughly convincing, but the actor sitting at the end of the bar, they all exclaimed, was excellent. It seemed to everyone watching that because of him an atmosphere of actually seeing the inside of a tavern with all its habitués pervaded the set and lent an aura of truth that emphasized the plot, the words, and actions of the two fine actors who were the focal point of attention. The director, too, was greatly intrigued by the extra whom he had given nothing more to do than to sit quietly nursing a single drink at the end of the bar.

The interesting aspect was that in each of the observer's eyes there was presented a different picture of the actor's ''inner'' life. The observers' imaginations were stimulated by the extra's demeanor and each saw a reality which related itself to the individual beholder. Some saw a man who had lost his job and was indulging in drink; a man thinking of his past and perhaps his hopeless future; others saw him struggling with himself as to whether he should have another drink; another saw a person just lost in mundane, contemplative thought. What was created was exactly what would happen if one tried to analyze a stranger sitting in a bar, not aware that he was being observed.

However, all agreed on one thing: Everyone watching the scene had seen real thoughts being created, thoughts so true that an invasion of them would have seemed disastrous and, that without them the ''tavern'' itself would disappear and revert to a vacuous stage setting. When the director inquired as to what the actor thought had produced this effect, he was told of the concentrated work he had done which had produced the clear and real attitude of the character.

The actor explained how he had taken, as a task, a simple book of matches and with his incredible concentration began first to silently ask himself a series of questions pertinent only to the book of matches.

He asked: What are the dimensions of the open folder of matches? After an appraisal had been made of the booklet in front of him, he decided it was approximately 2 inches wide, 3 inches long, and probably a millimeter thick.

What are they made from? Paper. Just simple paper, not unlike a lightweight cardboard.

Where did the paper come from? From trees originally. Trees that were cut down far away in forests, floated down streams and rivers, put on flatcars, and taken to a mill where they were pressed to a pulp, then chemically treated, and pressed again, somehow, into paper.

On and on his actor's imagination carried him, like the

logs floating downstream, following as far as a layman can the whole process of the production of the simple match folder.

Again he asked himself: How many words are printed on the cover? He counted them. 84 words.

From there he went to the little steel staple holding the matches to the folder and the machines needed for its manufacture and implementation, keeping his concentration on every aspect which his imagination could conjure. On he went to the dyes in the paper which color the advertisement, the printing of the words, the sulphur in the matchheads, following along with genuine thoughts as far as he could this whole, now wonderful, chain of events.

It is not difficult to imagine the real thought-expressions, the vividness of them, the life that was given to the character, and, consequently, to the scene itself. Without this one "simple task," as the actor called it, the opening scene of the play might have missed some of the dramatic impact it needed.

The actor in the above story knew his art well enough to realize that, even though his part was small, it was not small enough to prevent him from expressing the skill and artistry of his craft as he learned to do.

The question may now arise as to how an actor can attain that inner feeling, that inner life and spirit of a person who has committed an act which you as a person have never done. For instance, a murderer. How can one portray with realism all the positive forces, the complex, foreign, and incomprehensible nature of a person who takes the life of another? Let me say first that "life" is something which ranges from the most discernible objects such as mother, father, sister, trees, dog, birds, insects, and lichens to very intangible, often poetic, expressions of existence. We have all killed a living thing at some time in our lives; indeed many times.

Have you never at least killed a bug, a plant, a mouse, or an idea? Yes, even ideas live, though they are elusive and sometimes intangible. But this is not the same as murdering a human being you say! True, but here the actor makes use of what he has learned in order to *create a reality he has never known*, at least as is presented on a stage, a murderer's Inner Character. How this is done will depend largely on the individual actor for obviously this area of the character will be a most personal one and will result from the affinity developed to the task. We all have our special dislikes, peevishnesses, and hates. And if one in particular were personalized and strengthened in harmony and agreement with the plot of the play, the result would be the impression of one who hates enough to commit a murder. Then it only needs to be carried out on stage. The feelings of the character after the murder is committed would again depend upon the story line of the script.

The lines may state that the character is supposed to feel sorrowful for what he has done or may even say that the character is exultant over the deed. Whatever the inner feeling is, it will depend on the actor having an affinity to an experience which will produce a similar feeling in him and then proceeding to build it to its proper concentrated pitch. In both cases, the feeling leading to the murder and the resultant one after the murder, a Personalization could be used to great advantage to achieve the Inner Character. We have all committed cruel acts in life that we were sorry for after they were done. We also have done things at times when our lack of sympathy and display of feeling that approached sadism later amazed us. Whether we have killed a robin with an air rifle and felt deep remorse for the insensibility of the act as we watched the bird gasp its last breath or whether we voiced a crushing remark designed to hurt and then experienced a secret joy when we found it had done its work, it all amounts to the same thing when applied to the art of living. It simply means that we all possess to some varying degree the same qualities found in a man who could hurt enough to kill another man. The height to which these Personalizations can take us as actors depends on their strength and relationship to our psyche. If they are exceptionally strong, we need not have difficulty in attaining a degree of feeling as just discussed. The pleasurable thing to remember is that the audience never knows what you are thinking or from where your creation stems. All they see is the sheer artistry of your performance.

Personalizations are not the only method by which Inner Character is created. The above instance is only used as a typical example. The many, many different ways will vary with the individual actor and, also, with the literally thousands of different effects of shading, highlighting, colors, and with facets of the character. What will work for one actor may fail another and vice versa.

As an example of how Sense Memory itself can be employed for characterization, let us stay in the same vein of thought as with the murderer characterization, only now let us progress to the person who has been murdered. The act of moribundity is usually accepted by actors as being the easiest of all tasks to perform. They believe that all that needs to be done is to flop over, emit a groan, and then lie perfectly still. True, this is usually the way it is performed, but nothing could be further from reality when the situation actually occurs in life. There are many other things which happen to *cause* this effect. These are the ingredients usually left out by most actors. In the first place, dying is not an easy thing to do. By this I mean, taken from a purely clinical viewpoint, the human body does not find it easy to yield to the act itself. On the contrary, it resists through many battles involving its existence until thoroughly defeated. Even then, when death has clearly won, it always makes that gallant try to regain its lost life by the death rattle as though attempting to shake itself loose from death's ultimate grip.

Besides the factors just named in the act of dying, there are always the events which leap up to it. Let us take the case of a person who has been poisoned and demonstrate how the use of Sense Memory can create the primary steps which precede death and cause it. Again, the following is meant as an illustration and not as a dogmatic method for every actor to use. There are many formulas and an actor may find another to be more suitable to his instrument. We realize that murder is not created on stage by actually killing nor death by actually dying. Experiences such as these can be realistically done on stage by creating the physical sensory aspects that express the act. Whereas most actors resort to the taking of poison with facial grimaces, clutching the stomach, and gasping for breath, the effort should be on the series of events as they really occur in life, not as you might imagine in a conventional and general way. If we see a person die before us in life, we do not remain unaffected by the experience. Why do we so often remain so in the theatre?

Try the following two distinctly different Sense Memory exercises: With Sense Memory, taste a lemon, aspirin, alum, or any common substance that is mildly disagreeable to the taste; then do a Sense Memory exercise for a clearly defined pain. Do these two exercises together and the impression of poison being taken will clearly result. Remember, too, that if the character suddenly realizes what he has taken, there will be a sincere effort to clear the mouth of any remains. This in itself is a simple act, but the effect is a real one and can be quite startling. All of us at some time in our lives have taken something that "tastes like poison." Often this substance can be recreated to our sense of taste by Personalization or even an Affective Memory exercise if it was serious enough. So in addition to the use of Sense Memory per se, our Inner Characterization would now take this new task. Certainly there are many Affective Memory exercises in all of us to take care of strong and even extraordinary emotional experiences such as mentioned previously. But it is, of course, left up to the individual to chose which part of the Method is best-suited to the problem and to his instrument; which part can be trusted for truthful results; which part can be depended upon consistently night after night. These are acting problems that are best worked out during rehearsals. It is not uncommon for a Personalization to seem correct for a certain scene and later to discover it does not give the proper visage or the desired effects. It may also be discovered that the strength and lasting quality of an Affective Memory will work better. It is during rehearsals that such serious problems must be aligned correctly with the actor's instrument.

As in all forms of art, there inevitably exists in acting the time when the creative spirit, inspiration, or concentration is interfered with because whatever outside forces present are *overly* present by virtue of their strength may interfere with the tasks set for the creation of the role's Inner Character. When this happens, this actor finds that, try as he may, they usually resist successfully any effort to overcome them. Often it will only be a minor disturbance such as a cross word with a friend or an unpaid bill at the tailor's that will set off a chain reaction resulting in a partial or total loss of the tasks involved in the work. It can even be a happy event which seemingly whisks away all you have worked so hard for.

Now it would appear at first glance that the concentration is at fault in such a case. Possibly, but usually it involves more than just the concentration because the rest of the sensitive branches of the instrument have been disrupted causing any of the reality formerly attained to be lost. Therefore, regaining the concentration alone would be to no avail for it would not have the reality and logic of the scene to guide it. An experience such as this can be a most depressing thing, if not a frightening one.

At a time like this the actor must be able to permit the feeling (that is, the experience and emotions which are happening to him while on stage) to enter into his character and assume them. This is spoken of as *using the reality of your situation*. In other words, if at some time the actor's true feelings are stronger than the tasks he has set for himself, he must be able to use them as they occur. He must unhesitatingly allow them to flow into the character he is portraying, saying all the while the author's words, but through the reality of his own personal feelings and emotions. He must never try to repress them. If he does the results are not difficult to imagine.

On the other hand, if he allows the emotion to come out whatever it is, these results may certainly not be the same as the results worked for in rehearsals or the results from the performance the night before. But what will result will be words spoken out of genuine reality and not out of repressed, unconcentrated, negative feelings. They will be spoken with conviction and clarity of image. Perhaps the character was not supposed to express such a "shading" as this might produce, but it would be far more preferable for one night's performance than a spurious performance caused by the repressive "block."

We have learned that there is not just one certain way for a word to be intoned. Indeed, the same holds true for any amount of lines so long as what results does so because of an existent reality. Then, too, sometimes a very interesting "shade" of the character can develop out of this; one that permits an element of intrigue to interject itself into the character. Suppose the role is that of a person who is purported to be disinterested in a certain course of events as they unfold in the scene. This is a definite quality of the character. Now, in life we know that no one is ever completely disinterested in anything. For even an abnormal amount of disinterest would have to show a cause, a reason for the state of disinterest to this extreme degree. This might delve too deeply at this point into a psychoanalytical nature. Suffice it to say that the most serious persons have their nonsensical moments and capricious persons their contemplative moments.

If the actor portraying this role arrives at the theatre in a somewhat depressed state and uses this feeling honestly, the audience's immediate reaction would be one of curiosity and interest as to what is causing the character's depression, so real would it be. They would directly relate his feelings to the particular words of the play. The same new "shading" or highlight of the character would develop if the actor arrived on stage in an extremely cheerful mood and directly applied the author's words to this or to any outstanding mental and emotional state present in the real life of the actor at the time. To those actors reading this who have always believed that one performance must not vary from another, let me remind them that this is impossible just as much so as if it had been said that a person in life could not vary in his emotions and feelings and inner spirit ever again.

The ability to use the feelings he has at the time he is acting often aligns the actor with the role better than if he had attended a great deal of preparatory work.

A case in point was related by Paula Strasberg one afternoon when her husband was too ill to hold his classes and she conducted them for him. Paula, an enlightened woman who possessed an extraordinary curiosity, had invited Marlon Brando to dinner at their apartment shortly after the premiere of Budd Schulberg's *On The Waterfront*. She told how she waited until after dinner was finished and coffee and brandy were being served to insist, in her charming way, that Brando tell her, in detail, how he had worked for the Inner Character which so forcefully presented itself in Terry Malloy's character during the last ten minutes of Waterfront.

In this scene, Brando's character is beaten almost to a pulp by a gang of ruthless union thugs in full view of hundreds of onlookers. He then has to walk, crawl, or drag himself toward a cowed group of dockworkers as a means of defiance, if he has any left. If he can reach this group of men on his own two feet, the symbolism established by this highly symbolic film will be one of moral defeat for the union boss and support and victory for the exploited stevedores who, it is presumed, will forcibly resist them in the future. There is no doubt as to the brilliance of Brando's performance. The sheer physical pain, the fear, the anxiety as to what his actions might bring, and the hopes which rested on him were clearly shown with such pathos and sincerity in his character portrayal that there was hardly a dry eye in the theatre.

Naturally, Paula had to know. She had prepared herself all day for Brando's answer which would surely include a lengthy list of preparatory tasks judiciously and painstakingly worked out beforehand. Imagine her disappointment when he told her that he had not used a series of Affective Memories, Personalizations, Sense Memory, Physical Exercises, etc., but had instead used, simply and naturally, the feeling, both emotional and sensory, that he, Marlon Brando, had felt during the filming of the scene.

Paula's incredulity was surpassed only by her now intensified curiosity. How had he done it? What could possibly have taken place in his own personal life that day which he could use in such a horrifying scene and which would produce such a startlingly real performance?

Brando's answer lay in the fact that the scene had been besieged with a series of delays and retakes due to bad weather and technological difficulties. Filmed in Hoboken, New Jersey, on actual waterfront docks where adequate protection for the crew from the cold rain and biting wind was negligible, the end of the day approached with the important scene still not in the can. At last a break in the weather allowed the camera crew to set up the scene for shooting but by this time everyone including Brando was tired, irritable, and close to disgust. Wet from rain, cold and hungry after almost twelve hours of futile waiting with only sandwiches to eat all day, Brando allowed all of these sensory and emotional feelings to flow through his every action, word, and movement creating for the audience the torture and hell endured by the character. To have hidden his true feeling would have been impossible at the time, so he simply used the real ones which already existed and which he felt would fit the character perfectly. He was so right.

Though the actor may spend years in training his instrument, all of this training would be to no avail if the instrument did not assimilate additional training of which the actor sometimes is completely unaware. This additional training is assimilated by the many happenings of everyday life and our relationships to them. We can call on these directly for the reaction of our art and are fully conscious of their own origin. We know when to choose a past experience from our own life and to apply it directly to a role; we know how to create all the sensory aspects of a role (among many others). But sometimes there is another relationship to circumstances that we do not consciously express. One that we are hardly ever aware of when we try to relate our conscious mind to a foreign situation as the role of the murderer. Since man's subconscious plays a drastically important role in his conscious life, it would of course, influence the actor's instrument as well.

However, the importance that the subconscious plays in the actor's faith, his own personal justification and affinity with the inner character of a role, can be illustrated still further by recent theories of the medical and psychiatric world, theories which are fast becoming accepted facts. Modern medicine has advanced some of Freud's theories concerning dreams to the point where it is now believed that man's dreams greatly govern the rationality of his actions in his conscious life; for that matter, his very sanity. These dreams, often fantastic and bizarre, which everyone experiences but seldom can recall on awakening, give us free vent to expression; expression that we would never think of presenting in our wakeful life. In our dreams we are warriors brave and valiant, heroines, robbers, murderers, and lovers. We do things in our dreams that we would not admit to our closest friend and often will not admit to ourselves. The theory that our subconscious desires are released in dreams, thus preventing us from actually executing them in life which would be a manifestation of insanity, tends to prove itself through vast experiments. When a person is denied his dreams by a forcible awakening at the time they begin, he in turn tends to express them in his conscious life. This has been shown on many human volunteers by use of a brain wave machine which records dream beginnings to the scientists who in turn wake the person before his dream is fulfilled. He is then allowed to go back to sleep until the machine shows the beginning of another dream. This continues through the night, night after night. Results have shown the volunteer to take on irritable and often irrational and erratic behavior.

An important piece of the theory is presented to the actor: But for the presence of dreams he could very well become involved in situations that would otherwise be unthinkable to him; situations such as ones often presented by the author of a play! This alone is valuable to his actor's faith for it means that we all at one time or another in our dreams have committed crimes of violence and engaged in activities which we could not fathom doing in life but which were certainly done with complete mental, though subconscious, reality while sleeping; living through every phantasmal moment as though it were actually happening. From the premise of this theory, we can even draw a close line to the Inner Character of a role and to our own Inner Character. The fact that we are seldom able to remember all of our muddled dreams should be proof enough that it would be too much of a shock to our sensibilities to realize or accept that we dreamed such things. Nature has a way of obliterating unpleasantness by dimming our memories but, by the same token, she has her own way of not being repressed as is evidenced by our dreams.

Another interesting aspect of this proposition is that our actor's instrument is being trained, not only by the happenings in everyday life, but also, while we sleep. It is, of course, a kind of training that needs conscious awareness and further conscious preparatory training in order to pluck it from its depths but, nevertheless, it is there ever ripening and waiting for the actor's imagination to utilize it. I mention this strictly as a means of strengthening the actor's faith and as an aid in attaining the wealth of imagination and personal belief needed in his role; a faith that tells him first of all that he can supply what his role calls for.

Developing the Inner Character of a role often demands a sincerity and devotion to the actor's art that is very rare in the theatre today. Because of this rarity, a great amount of theatrical realism, to say nothing of healthy theatrical tradition, is irretrievably lost. In order to be able to maintain the powerful inner life of his character, the actor must prepare his instrument, his thinking and reasoning, far enough in advance to first assimilate the character to his instrument. A good example of the extent to which a dedicated artist of the past prepared himself for his role is seen in Eleanor Ruggles' book, *Prince of Players*. She describes Junius Booth, the leading Shakespearean actor of his day, who was the father of Edwin and John Wilkes. "All through the morning and afternoon he lived the character he was to play that night. Somebody once offered him a pork sandwich on a Shylock day. He snatched the meat out and threw it on the floor, 'Infidel dog!' "

It stands to reason that if the actor allows himself no time during the day to prepare for his role that night, if he races about performing inane and capricious acts with his valuable time and never thinks of his role until a few minutes before his entrance on stage, a great part of his art, if not all, will be soon vitiated and the miasmal craters of conventionality will swallow it.

The actor's preparation for his role should not start with his entrance into the dressing room or on his trip to the theatre. It should begin long before his arrival at the theatre; even as early as his awakening of the day. The preliminary tasks solved in his characterization, accomplished by a mental picture of his character, will be stimulated by his awareness of all that abounds in life around him. He must take advantage of life's little intricacies to discover new realities in his character and by learning how his character would react to a given situation. As for actual stage tasks, he must allow himself more than enough time for their preparation.

If for example, his character in the play is supposed to make his entrance after having gone without sleep for two days and nights, the actor must retrace, first mentally, then physically by means of the senses, all that took place in the character's life those two days and nights, then making the necessary adjustments which will apply to him personally. He must bring with him on stage the physical weariness, the ache in the legs, arms, shoulders, the pain in his eyes from too much light in the room, the lack of mental alertness, fuzzy or tired speech, his strained walk, and vacant expression; anything that is as the actor himself would express it in life.

Enough has been emphasized earlier to determine that the work involved in full creation of Inner Character is not a simple task, though it can be an enjoyable one to the serious actor. It takes full preparation and this cannot be attained five minutes before curtain time.

Therefore, the actor must learn to adopt strict rules for himself and his night's work. He must avoid being distracted or disturbed while in the theatre. When in his dressing room, he must enter into his character by transferring all of his personal thoughts, thoughts not even related to the theatre, to the role itself for here begins the final culmination of his art. He will give another name, another character, his gift of life.

Creating the
Outer Character

The Outer Character of a role is simply the continuation of Inner Character creation. It is the culminating factor of all the mental and physical problems that have finally yielded to the actor's instrument and are now presented visually to the beholder.

In this chapter the subject of Outer Character will be centered on uniting all phases of the Method to form this visual impression and, also, on the proper attitude of objectivity which leads to originality in one's interpretation. It is this latter phase that so often confounds the young artist. To be able to give the freshness of originality to a role, while at the same time living the life of your character, is sometimes not an easy thing to do. All too often we fall into the depths of conventional acting without first trying to discern how a role can be made fresh and alive. Then, too, we often miss the originality that seems to accompany that which is real; that which is constantly happening in life around us.

Actors are too content in the use of technique that has long since been regarded as cliché-acting by serious and dedicated students of the theatre. So, the question arises as to why they are satisfied with mediocrity instead of excellence. The answer is not to be found in a single example, although many acting teachers would proclaim verbosely that insensitivity and plain laziness on the actor's part would be inclusive in answering the question. In many cases, this may be true but certainly not all-inclusive. There are other factors involved, ranging from the history of acting through the various periods of "style" to the present day dissension with problems inherent in just getting a play on the boards or a movie in the "can." Then, of course, there are many complex psychological factors that present themselves because of the insecurity of our times and a certain reluctance on the part of the Western artist to portray even himself as he really is in life. This last observation is not by any means limited to the actor alone. Indeed, it is all too prevalent in directors, extending finally to the real power wielders, the producers and commercial elements who rule the kind of acting and direction to be seen in movies, or television, and, sometimes, on the legitimate stage. It is the weakness and lack of artistic insight on the part of not only many actors, but to a great extent to the people higher up in a position to give the world the full spiritual, artistic, and morally uplifting values of truly fine theatre. It has only been a matter of a few years (and by no means still universal), that one could enter a movie house and see the hero wearing something else besides the spotlessly clean white hat and the villain a dirty, shabby black sombrero. Symbolically, the hero was pure, therefore whitebedecked, extending to his remaining wardrobe and even to his horse. And, of course, the reverse had to be true of the villain. He was always of an unattractive mold and with greasy clothes, unshaven and unkempt face and beard, and mangy horse which, of course, could never outrun its white stallion counterpart.

Obviously, such Outer Character stylization has no contact with reality. Anyone knowing the slightest details concerning the life of the early American cowpoke realizes he was far from scrupulously clean in body hygiene. To see his immaculate white stetson, symbolic trademark of his purity and integrity, remain perched immovably atop his fair head while he battles innumerable odds is at best hokum and fantasy. If it were billed as such, it might not be so bad but unfortunately this is but a typical example of that which still passes as art. This is the sort of "art" that has run rampant in Hollywood for years and thankfully, due to a renaissance in acting, shows signs of dying out. Not that it dies easily for the obsequious usurpers of our nation's artistic taste and spiritual strength are constantly filling the air waves and theatres across the country with entertainment that is at best mediocre.

Movies with a western locale have increased steadily since their beginning but have in the past few years become not quite so hard to believe and, therefore, more palatable to the public taste. Movie making has in turn become an art form in the highest sense instead of just a means of providing cheap entertainment for the public. They have begun in the last ten years to drop their puerile ways and to show the first real signs of maturity. This is evidenced by the continued progress in realistic films; ones that possess the vitality and originality of life, both in the acting and in the screenplays and direction.

The Outer Character of a role, that which is generally seen first by the audience, should be the last problem taken to task by the actor. This is not due necessarily to the ease and facility of it but more because of the Outer Character's dependency on the inner life and spirit of the role. Too often the actor will plan in advance what his character will wear, how he will speak and react before the inner life of the role is formulated. In life outer manifestations are the result of feelings and the inner spirit of a person and it is this inner life which serves as a stimulus to forming the Outer Character. There is no other real basis for it. And so it must be on stage. The actor must discern *why* his character dresses the way he does and then set about to do so as he really would if the character existed in life. The latter is the difficult part because here the danger of slipping into conventionality resides.

We recalled earlier the conventional and obviously false dress and unlikely situations, etc., the early western movies centered on their heroes. (I say early when in reality they did not begin to disappear earlier than the 1950s. Actually, there are plenty of them still being filmed.) Let us now switch to the part of the villain. Not the one in the wild west movie, though many of these old flickers are being re-run via television, but instead to the villain with more contemporary characteristics. That of the modern day hoodlum, gangster, or "syndicate" mobster who is portrayed just as virulently and frequently as was the "bad man" of yesteryear.

Examine what is usually seen in the portrayal. First, the actor portrays the way he thinks a person on the outskirts of law and order would behave. He makes him speak out of the side of his mouth with a rough sort of speech, he plays him as arrogant, ignorant, and illiterate and resorts to every known cliché which to the public's now-conditioned mind, seems to typify this sort of character. Worst of all, he makes him obvious. Nothing could be further from reality for if all mobsters were as obvious as actors usually portray them, it would only be a matter of hours before law enforcement agencies would eliminate all crime in the nation. Does it not stand to reason that if the audience can spot the villain from the very beginning, the other characters in the play, if they really existed in life, would be able to do the same thing? Therefore, from one such false portrayal can come many false portrayals. It can literally entrap every actor playing opposite him. If the character behaved in life the way he does on stage, he would be recognized as such immediately, thus drawing forth truthful reactions to his behavior. But on stage, the rest of the cast playing opposite him is restrained from this recognition by the script which says that he is not to be recognized for what he is. How, then, can truthful reactions come from the actors playing opposite him?

This is a problem that is common among writers as well as actors for they too do not bother to draw such important characterizations from life.

Many actors feel that a character such as just described has to "show" the audience what he really is or else they will miss it. This is where the actor makes his first mistake. There is an old saying: "Give everybody else credit for having as much sense as you have," which certainly applies here. Audiences are smarter and more sophisticated today then ever before and it takes a very intricate and complex script to fool them for even a little while. It is only when a character can behave like everyone else and then turn out to be different that he stimulates interest to the audience. For this is the way it is in life. It is always the contrast that is interesting.

So then, the problem seems to be one of not being obvious; of not giving the plot away, so to speak. The actor must remember that in life the underworld figure does not try to be obvious; he does not try to act like a gangster. The reverse is also true of the innocent; he does not try to behave as one who is naive but, instead, as one who is worldly. The above problem is one that is prevalent in the acting of Shakespeare's plays. The stress should be on reality more than anything else in his plays. Too often reality is discarded for voice, diction, stance, movement, and other superficial aspects of the characters. Some Shakespeare zealots will say that the beauty of his plays lies in his speech. True, his language, speech, and poetry is beautiful, but the way to make them beautiful on stage is not to rely on the words alone. You cannot play beauty on stage any more than you can work for the end result per se. It is only when Shakespeare's characters are made to come alive as real people that the beauty of their speech becomes really evident.

Yet, too many actors feel that their characters must be made obvious to the audience when in reality the reverse is true. How often we leave a performance of *Othello* and hear the audience remark, "Iago certainly looked like a villain." A villain is precisely what Iago should not look like. We cannot help wondering that if he were so obvious, why would Othello not recognize him for what he was? Othello was far from being a stupid man.

To return to the role of a modern gangster or hoodlum, it is very tempting to portray him in an obvious light; possibly because it gives the actor a chance to change himself so much. He may affect a particular stance which he thinks reflects that of a tough guy; he will change his speech to sound rough and crude; he will insist on the worst imaginable taste in the clothes to be worn as his costume (taste which the actor thinks a character such as this would have). (Probably subconsciously if not consciously, he knows that he as an actor will stand out more conspicuously garbed in such a manner.) It is not uncommon to see such a character outfitted in a loud striped suit, wide-brimmed hat as worn in the 1920s, pointed shoes, cheap jewelry, and, of course, the most obvious of all, the black shirt and white tie. What the actor does not realize is that this sort of wardrobe went out of style probably forty years ago and even if it hadn't it would hardly be worn by a person who above all does not wish to draw unnecessary attention to himself. A man who in real life is an underworld figure does not try to behave like one in public. The one thing he craves more than anything else is respectability, if not as a personal desire then at least to avoid detection. Consequently, he does everything in his power to attain this, short of giving up his chosen profession. He buys good conservative clothes and sports these as proof of his respectability. It is here that the reality of the situation can be presented to the audience without being too obvious and indicating, because often a person like this might make a slight mistake in his attire.

Picture him with his beautifully cut suit, subdued black shoes, and expensive hat. But instead of a conservative shirt to match, he dons a long-collared white-on-white silk shirt either because of personal taste in his past life or the expense and will be completely unaware of committing an error in dress. Thus, the conservative effect is lost in his wardrobe. If not the shirt, it may be one of a thousand things chosen with imagination by the actor.

Now let us suppose that he is too smart for this. Picture him as having infinite sartorial taste in everything he purchases for his wardrobe. Suits, shirts, ties, hats, shoes, and socks, everything is correct. He also knows that the respectable business man with good taste chooses conservative jewelry. So he buys a plain gold wristwatch with matching band. If he so desires he will purchase a perfectly plain gold identification bracelet or a gold ring with a nice conservative stone such as a garnet; maybe even one with a crest embossed on it and perhaps, if he likes, both. Next he needs a nice conservative tie pin, not a diamond one but maybe a black pearl. Then cufflinks, collar pin, and even lapel stud. We need go no further. What does he do? What is his little mistake? He wears everything together on the same outing and by so doing lends a feeling of suspicion and possibly, at the same time, interest and vitality to the character. In this way, the character is presented more realistically with regard to background and training in respectability. This is a good example of the imagination that can be employed by the actor. However, these instances reflect only the type of character who by virtue of the script is supposed to be placed under suspicion and surveillance by the rest of the cast and the audience. For while he may come under suspicion, he need not be the obvious stereotype gangster that everyone recognizes immediately.

Usually a simple device is enough for the audience to realize what is happening and in the above case all the trouble that the character has gone through to hide his real self is more than sufficient. A gangster would strive toward respectability in his clothing and the same holds true for his speech. The thing for an actor to keep in mind is that his character tries to speak correctly, not improperly, as so many actors tend to do. This is where the actor's emphasis should lie: To make his character *try* to speak properly, not incorrectly. This is the way it would be in life. But again, all too often the actor tries to speak badly as the character and the result does not sound natural.

Now suppose that the gangster spoke letter-perfect with the exception of one little word that was mispronounced or accented with an unmistakable mark of having originated in an earlier, more undesirable environment. This would not mean he was a gangster of course, but it would inject interest into that part of his life which is not revealed in the script. A simple Physical Exercise for a conflict in the speech can be utilized for the Outer Character just as was shown by Michael Wager's interpretation of the Dauphin in Shaw's *Saint Joan*. These are just a few of the truths that can be inculcated into the Outer Character in order to exhibit him in the actor's original and realistic light. They are used to illustrate that the simplicity of reality is far more interesting than contrived, unnatural characterizations. It is in the contrast of a person's demeanor that this fact is graphically demonstrated. The evil of a man's character can be made more vivid and realistic by highlighting his good qualities and for this reason the actor must search far beyond the author's usual description for his characterization. When a script states that the character is good, the actor must look for his faults, his little human weaknesses. When he is ill, he must find where he is well and healthy. Only by contrast, and not playing only one aspect of the character, will his role become alive and fairly breathe truth on stage. We know in life that a true hero is no more perfect than anyone else. Neither is he always tall, dark, and handsome. Conversely, villains in life are rarely obvious in their villainy. Indeed, it is often their attractiveness that hides their true nature and then highlights their evilness when discovered. As the actor delves deeper into his character, he must always emerge to grasp the simple truths of life and adapt them to his instrument. Many are as subtle as rustling leaves but when uncovered are as powerful as the strongest wind and can carry the life of the character into the hearts and minds of the audience where it will remain forever.

Two examples of how the Outer Character of a part is affected by one's training can be elucidated best by work I have seen done. The two actresses involved are entirely different "types." The first, known for talents which pursue the classics and very serious drama, the second, known equally well but accepted by the public as having had a talent which ran no deeper than her own generous physical endowments. One whose instrument has had stilted, formal training but who has overcome the inevitable by talent alone; the other an actress who had not experienced any training until she came to Lee Strasberg to study but was already at the peak of international stardom when she abandoned Hollywood for her studies.

Now, my first brush with a professional acting career began with summer stock at the world famous Barter Theatre of Virginia. This was also before my studies of the Method began and I think, because of the work seen at this venerable old theatre, my interest in the need of a method of sorts was stimulated. While there, it was my good fortune to land a small but salient role played directly with Dame Judith Anderson in *Family Portrait* by Lenore Coffee and William Joyce Cowan.

I still feel a certain awe for the pure, innate technique displayed by Dame Judith. Her technique was, of course, comprised of all the traditional training of the English stage with great emphasis placed on diction, voice, enunciation, elocution, pronunciation, and formalized stage presence and administered by strict discipline and rules of conduct which even included some rather outdated stage superstitions. (The latter being no whistling in the dressing rooms, never wishing a fellow actor "Good luck," but instead "Break a leg!" never passing anyone while descending or ascending a flight of stairs and never delivering the tag line of a play at any rehearsal.) It is important to note that in spite of such unrealities surrounding her "old school" training, her undeniable talent persistently shone in every performance I saw. The incongruity of her training and personal beliefs still could not deter her remarkably beautiful performances. Watching her last scene from the wings, where I was asked to hold a piece of curtain to shield her from the view of the audience between curtain calls, gave me the opportunity to observe closely the extent of her seemingly deep feelings about her role of Mary, the mother of Jesus. This last scene never failed to evoke tears from my eyes as it did hers and to this day the same feeling, tears, and pity flow forth from me at the slightest recall of the scene.

In this scene, which takes place after Jesus has been crucified, Mary and Jesus' youngest brother, Juda, are awaiting the imminent birth of Juda's first child. They are sitting on the front porch of the house that was the main setting when from inside the house the crying of a newborn babe is heard.

As Juda starts to dash into the house, Mary stops him and asks a favor. She asks Juda that if the baby is a boy would he mind naming him after his brother, clarifying that she means his oldest brother, Jesus. Juda replies that he would be glad to do so and that he will speak to his wife about it. He then disappears inside the house. Only a few moments lapsed before Miss Anderson slowly rose from her chair. She silently walked down the porch steps, out into the front "yard" of the house which was close to the stage apron and the footlights, and delivered the last line in a seemingly inaudible whisper; a whisper spoken from the bereavement that comes from a mother's supreme loss and one directed to the innermost confines of her own heart. With tears streaming down her cheeks, her soft whisper was heard in the rafters to say, "I wouldn't want his name to be forgotten."

Needless to say, there was not a dry eye in the theatre, out front or backstage. As I have stated before, Dame Judith Anderson is one of those extremely rare and gifted individuals who by virtue of outer technique and will, which she later informed me, can bring forth tears at any desired time. The number of artists in the world who can foster such emotion purely at will could probably be counted on the fingers of one hand. Yet, she is still a unique example of one's innate talents reigning supreme over the type of training which produces much of the stilted acting today. For anyone but her, the range of emotional feelings in this play would be a formidable challenge to any actress living today. However, she made it look like child's play. The extent of her purely superficial technique was demonstrated to me after one performance on a particularly hot and humid matinee day. She had just made her final exit and was standing behind the curtain I held to conceal her from the audience, waiting to take her bows. She turned to me in an agitated manner and snapped, "How damned hot it is in this bloody theatre!" Nevertheless, my awesome reverence of her performance as Mary, the mother of our Lord, was only slightly shaken.

The next rather surprising bit of acting with equally unexpected results regarding Outer Character form concerns the first scene that Marilyn Monroe did in Lee Strasberg's class. Contrary to popular belief that she was admitted as a member of the Actors' Studio when she first arrived in New York, Marilyn enrolled in Strasberg's private classes which are separate and apart from the Actors' Studio, undoubtedly as a paying student like anyone else. Whereas the tuition for the private classes would be a nominal amount for the majority of the students, the Actors' Studio runs on a free scholarship basis for every member. A series of rigid auditions must be passed to gain entrance to the Studio, but in the case of Strasberg's private classes the desire to act and the necessary fee is usually all that is required. This is not to say that he accepts all applications. It is true that Marilyn was permitted to attend several classes at the Studio, but strictly as an observer, as are others from time to time. Her attendance in Lee's private classes was very good and she seemed to take an avid interest in every scene performed by her fellow actors and in every word of criticism and instruction offered by Strasberg. Most students after enrolling can hardly wait to choose a partner in the classes and begin work on a scene, a play, or an edited novel, or a short story and to have their work picked apart by Strasberg. Being an extremely shy and reticent individual, Marilyn Monroe rarely raised a question concerning the work in progress. She was content to sit and watch and to occasionally jot down a note or two. Months passed but a scene from Marilyn was still not forthcoming.

Finally a whole year lapsed and word was that Lee had definitely spoken to her privately and informed her that she should be doing some scene work. Let me explain here that Lee's classes are divided into two types of study for every student with one day per week devoted to scene work (that is, actually acting a scene in front of Lee and the class), and one day per week spent on exercises intended for the training of the instrument. Marilyn had been keeping up with her exercise work and had been progressing nicely, but as I say had not once attended acting a scene with a fellow student until a full *eighteen months* had passed.

At last, word circulated among Strasberg's three or four

sets of classes that "Monroe" had finally decided to do a scene. When the day came nearly every student from all his classes jammed the little theatre that he leased to conduct his classes. There must have been two hundred students in an auditorium designed to hold a third that number.

I think I should interject here some of the intriguing aspects of Marilyn's enrollment with Strasberg before continuing with the outcome of her scene. In the first place, there was a great deal of resentment and even open antagonism directed toward Marilyn and Strasberg personally by dedicated and idealistic students who considered themselves to be head and shoulders above any "import" from Hollywood. This was especially true in the mid 1950s when Marilyn was regarded by students and the public alike as the antithesis of everything Strasberg and the Actors' Studio represented. She was at her zenith as an internationally known celluloid sex symbol—nothing more—and the world's press made much copy when news leaked of her proposed New York studies with Lee Strasberg. Some Strasberg students actually thought that he had gone a little soft in the head while others believed he was losing his idealistic values and was succumbing to the auspicious publicity and resounding acceptance that he and his work had begun to enjoy only in the past few years. None of these speculations could have been more contrary to fact. The truth was that Lee had from the beginning a very strong faith in Marilyn's potential as an actress of greater depth than she had hitherto shown on the screen. For reasons of his own, he believed hers was a talent that had been completely misguided, misdirected, and mischannelled all of her professional life. He often erupted with these convictions whenever anyone dared hint that he might be letting himself in for adverse criticism from outside sources as well as "at home" in his classes and at the Studio.

Marilyn chose a scene from Clifford Odets' play *Golden Boy,* and played the part of Lorna Moon opposite a particularly fine acting student named Philip Roth who portrayed the role of the fight manager. Without going to the actual dialogue of the scene or trying to give specific actions which occurred according to the plot, I would rather give the reader a mental impression of the Outer Character which Marilyn manifested throughout the entire thirty-minute scene.

The crowded classroom was anxious for it to begin and the atmosphere was one similar to attendance of a premiere. As the scene opened on Marilyn in the apartment furnished her by her shady boyfriend, all attention concentrated on her. The first few minutes were occupied by creating sensory tasks; various objects in the room which were not available as props and, also, the definite all-prevailing sense of stifling heat in an apartment on a hot summer day. It was obvious that she had taken plenty of time before the scene began to completely relax in order for her concentration to work correctly.

Often in the beginning of one's work with the Method, a highly likely and perfectly natural occurrence takes place in the work and Marilyn was no exception. The concentration on the tasks (in other words, the work itself), is just as evident as the results the actor is working for. Nevertheless, only seconds after the lines of the scene began with the appearance of her partner, did the first beads of perspiration become noticeable. Here was the first sign that she was applying the Method toward using her instrument correctly!

It should be pointed out here that sometimes perspiration develops because of nervousness. However, perspiration never develops if nervousness is present at the time a person is trying to create the heat. The nervousness would completely negate the concentration and prevent the "heat" from being created. It was fairly obvious to everyone that she was fully relaxed and her instrument was working beautifully.

From then on the crowded little room was as silent as a tomb while visitors from the Actors' Studio and Lee's other classes watched every movement issue forth from the warm, oppressive atmosphere her instrument had created. Next, the entire classroom seemed to be aware of her voice; a voice that while sounding perfectly natural with truthful inflection and meaning, did not sound at all like the voice heard from so many movie theatres. About halfway through this scene everyone seemed to realize that they were seeing a Marilyn Monroe that the whole world had never seen. They were seeing her as she really was, the Marilyn Monroe who only in the privacy of her own room could behave in such a real manner. Here was a woman; not a symbol of something which does not exist in reality. Here also was the play's character: A woman with the strength of a real woman; a woman who was nothing more than a harlot, a hustler, a conniver of the first order but one who had finally been overwhelmed by a feeling of genuine love for the first time in her life. Here was the role of a woman trying to break with the past; the gangster, the rottenness of her whole life. These were the things we saw in the scene.

She used her real self completely in the scene and with this intrinsic insight she suited the role perfectly. The perceptiveness she displayed proved she had worked diligently and thoroughly. Gone were the strained efforts of artificial behavior and clichés. Gone were the puckered lips, the swinging hips, the "little girl" voice that insensitive entrepreneurs had nurtured and fostered for a decade. She held nothing back. The feeling that had long epitomized her as an artificial performer who sold sex on the screen through sham behavior which lacked any inner basis of reality disappeared before our eyes. The feeling that one gets when seeing something he does not truly believe, the feeling of being cheated and usually being loathe of it, disappeared too.

The false sexiness was gone, and in its place, an interest in the problems of the character she portrayed. Gone also from the minds of the actors watching the scene was the preconceived idea about her, her talents, her capabilities, and her potential.

Among artists and the public alike who have always scorned her acting, I believe the basis for their scorn has been a deep feeling or suspicion that Marilyn Monroe had the ability to give them what they expected to see in art, but never fully saw. It is because they had caught only glimmerings of her potential that they felt cheated to an extent. She had always held back in everything she had done in life; but that afternoon in class her sensitivity, the character's problems, feelings, and emotions and every aspect of Marilyn Monroe as a real live human being seemed to be not inside her but hovering, encircling outside her body and functioning in the Outer Character of Lorna Moon. In her scene a perfect example was afforded to a large group of actors of how all the inner functions of the character serve to continue until the Outer Character is fully created.

However, the most important aspect of the scene came from her own natural behavior. This was stimulated from working correctly on the Inner Character and letting it flow through the Outer Character. By virtue of this we all knew that we were watching a Marilyn Monroe the world had never known or seen. Probably the most striking thing about the scene outside of the wonderful natural quality present in her voice (one we had never heard) was the ease of movement on stage. I suppose everyone in class that day was expecting to see the famous Marilyn Monroe ''wiggle'' as she moved about the stage. But no. Here was just a girl, an ordinary girl who moved like everyone else. And yet, at the same time all the truthful characteristics of Marilyn, the ones we all suspected subconsciously that she possessed, were very evident.

When their scene was finished, Marilyn and Phil sat down in two chairs close to the edge of the stage so as to hear clearly Lee's criticism. There remained a stunned silence on the part of the observers. It was a pleasant silence though because the realization was that Strasberg had lost none of his fantastic perception and judgment. Before beginning his long critique of the scene, Lee could not resist turning full way around in his front row seat, facing the entire assemblage and asking, or rather demanding, ''Well, was the scene excellent or not?'' To this the answer was resoundingly unanimous in the affirmative.

As an afterthought since her tragic death, it may be wondered when she would have fully applied her talents. True, her work in the last three or four films she made showed definite improvement over all the other films she made. This improvement came after she abandoned the ''Hollywood'' phase of her career and seriously began to study her craft. Also, she did prove herself to a hard core group of critics in Strasberg's class. She proved what she could do if she wanted to and that is something many actors never do. But then again she always moved slowly. After all, it took her eighteen months to do a scene for Strasberg's class so we might have had quite a long wait before seeing what she could really have done professionally. The sad part is that we all thought she had time.

The Outer Character of a role is that aspect which comprises all the phases of the work and presents them to the audience visually. Everything previously discussed is manifested in the Outer Character. Many of the problems accompanying Outer Character can be traced directly *inward* to the Inner Character.

For example, directors are often troubled by awkwardness on the part of actors when playing love scenes. In a love scene which is usually a powerful part of any drama, troubles arise when the actors say they do not know where to place their arms, their hands, or how to hold their partner. It is strange that these problems never exist in life! But all too often the naturalness and ease which are requisite for such a scene are lacking. Does it not stand to reason that if the two actors' inner feelings and spirit of their roles were functioning correctly there would be no need to even be directed in such a scene; that their movements and actions would innately solve any basic problems such as the placement of arms and hands? Next the actor must always keep in mind the type of play in which he is performing and ally this with the picture he already has of Outer Character. Again it is important to stay away from that which is obvious. If the play is a comedy, the Outer Character must possess a certain amount of contrast of emotions and behavior in order to highlight the comedy aspect. Therefore, the actor must not try to make the audience laugh constantly. *The logic of the illogic* presents itself when the director and the actor realize that the more serious and sincere the character, the funnier he will be by virtue of the situations and lines developed by the author. It is his sincerity which creates the comedy aspect.

In closing this chapter I feel that all actors must be urged to faithfully examine and re-examine, if necessary, their parts minutely in order to avoid falling into entrapments of obvious, conventional, stultifying behavior, no matter how well-performed. The artist in all fields must avoid the temptation to reproduce only appearances.

Likewise, he must not be obsessed with striving for beauty, per se. He must attain within the confines of his art all the force of life which lies therein and strive to produce faithfully through his instrument the elements needed for his art. Beauty should not be the goal of the artist but rather truth, originality, and vitality. From these come beauty of the highest order.

Social Mannerisms

Much has been said throughout this book on the need for actors to have keen awareness and sharp perception. It is as necessary for an actor to possess these traits as it is for a skilled draftsman to have blueprints. Without them he would be unable to study and understand the variations of life's *rara avis*, nature's laws, and the wealth of material from which to draw the basic characterizations required by his art. Conversely, he would also be unaware of himself and his own behavior. This is perhaps the most important reason for the need of perception and awareness. He must be able to analyze his own actions and gestures (whatever they are and no matter how trivial and at any time). He must be able to stop in the middle of any task in his own life and ask himself why he made a particular movement or sound, what motivated it, and then arrive at a truthful conclusion.

There are thousands of motions that the hands, feet, eyes, nose, fingers, shoulders, in short, the whole body go through of which the average individual is totally unaware and in which he is usually not interested. However, with actors it must be different. They must learn from other people what the motivating factors are that produce these seemingly meaningless movements. They must learn that the unspoken word is a powerful one and will be "spoken" even if not with sound. Serious actors realize this to be but another step toward creating the inner life of the character. But this awareness must also apply to the actor himself. Many actors have disconcerting mannerisms which they carry onto stage "in character." Often these can be irritating and distracting to the audience. These enigmatic, cacophonic *social mannerisms*, as they are called, can only be corrected in the actor's instrument by a conscious awareness of them. Naturally, we are aware of these mannerisms in other people before we notice them in ourselves. Therefore, it is in our close attention to other human beings that we find their hidden motivations as well as our own.

One marvel of nature is her ability to take over for us when we are unable to cope with the forces around us. This is pointedly demonstrated to the astute observer whenever feelings of insecurity are present in an individual. Usually accompanying this insecurity is the lack of conscious awareness that protection of some kind is needed and it is at this point that nature does her job. Have you ever been standing talking to someone and discovered that the only comfortable position you can find for yourself is with your arms folded across your chest? The person speaking to you may not be saying anything openly derogatory to you but something in his voice, his manner, his intonation, or maybe even his carriage has instinctively put you on your guard causing you to cross your arms and provide yourself with a symbolic shield, all without ever knowing it.

Sometimes a child placed in a strange room with adults, or even other children, will sink deeply into a chair until his shyness, which was probably caused by insecurity, disappears. Adults, too, will sit in a chair in such a way that it seems they are trying to get under the upholstery and form a barrier for the parts of their body most prone to actual physical attack. With a woman, however, sometimes the gesture of folding her arms across the chest is indicative of her own feelings about her breasts. She may make them feel less conspicuous by this motion or she may be in a better position to protect them or she may even use this action to support them—the latter either for physical relief or perhaps to lift them to better prominence.

You might be talking with a person and suddenly become

aware that he is buttoning his coat while listening to you. Under ordinary circumstances he may be seeking a defense. He is, at best, in a sense withdrawing from you or what you are talking about. A woman who finds herself ill at ease will behave much the same way depending upon the clothing she is wearing. If she is wearing a blouse, her fingers will clutch the opening at her throat and hold it closed with hardly a noticeable gesture to you or herself.

A gesture of escaping unpleasantness is commonly seen when a person places his hands partly over his eyes. Actually he is shielding the unpleasant object from his view and subconsciously he is saying, "If I can't see the object, it can't hurt me." The slight, almost imperceptible gesture is sometimes a dead giveaway to a person's inner feelings. For this reason, the actor's ability to discern the true meaning behind these actions is of paramount importance in his ever increasing search for truth and reality. This discernment must be applied not only to social mannerisms but, also, to speech and "slips of the tongue."

Freud believed that there were no "slips of the tongue"; that when allowed to grow careless in their speech people would say what their inner feelings dictated. The social attitudes in our society are such that truth and reality are sometimes disregarded for social niceties but, fortunately, nature does not recognize these "niceties" and will manifest herself in spite of them.

A person who constantly sits in a chair with his legs tightly crossed or his hands folded deeply in his lap gives other common indications of one who is seeking a defense to insecurity. I once knew a theatrical agent who indicated his feeling of insecurity through the arrangement of his office furniture. He sat behind a huge desk opposite his small staff with his back to the wall and with filing cabinets banked on either side. He had left a small space to be used as a passageway. Some of his past dealings with actors might have prompted more than just a subconscious feeling of insecurity and need for defensive measures.

As is often the case at social gatherings such as parties

where nearly everyone is a stranger, the desire to belong, to "fit in," is obvious if one knows where to look. A person seems to be sitting complacently in a chair but his uneasiness will appear by the way he folds and unfolds his hands as he subconsciously tries to "hold onto" the situation. When this person rises to cross the room, he will trail one hand innocently and lightly touch each object in his path seemingly to get stability and support from them. The agent I mentioned also kept on his desk-like barricade a wide assortment of papers, contract forms, and photographs of famous stars, all piled high in disarray. In this way he kept reassuring himself of his own importance to every actor who called upon him and could see such famous people carelessly scattered all over his desk.

Uncertainty is a common occurrence to everyone at some time in his life. All of us have doubts as to our own abilities but we do not always express them openly. We keep them hidden, bottled up inside of us. We often answer affirmatively to questions regarding our potential when in reality we may have grave doubts and uncertainties about it. Possibly, if a person hesitates in stating his own capabilities he knows he might lose a job or a big order for his company, so he says, "Why sure I can handle it." But the doubt may still be there. Nature again takes over and she will not be suppressed. A man who on the surface is full of assurance regarding his capabilities may make several gestures that belie his words. Running his fingers over that part of his face he shaves and feeling the stubble is his way of assuring himself that he is man enough to do what is required of him. The same need for assurance can be seen in the man who regularly runs his hands through his hair or even over a bald head. The need for assurance and the feeling of doubt is there.

As should be evident now, a person's hands are used extensively in betraying his words. He will use them to slightly cover his mouth when unsure of a statement; each finger slightly emphasizing each word as it is muttered to lend assurance. It is because of these rather nervous mannerisms, and the motivation lying behind them, that we do not always

believe what we hear even over his most sincere protesta-
tions. We may not know exactly why we doubt a person
except for the fact that nature's laws of truth work both ways
by giving us the innate ability to recognize truth if we look
for it.

I do not like to use the word intuition as it brings to mind
mystical qualities. However, intuition has a definite natural
foundation which is a form of perceptivity through *unconscious* awareness. We are after something more tangible and
more dependable than that. We must have *conscious* awareness.

We have all met people that we were drawn to on first
introduction; people with whom we immediately hit it off
from the very start of our acquaintanceship. This is not to
say that the initial relationships with these people will still
prevail at a later date but, nevertheless, at first introduction
a mutual bond of agreeableness and trust was present. This
attitude is probably the easiest to recognize. When one dis-
plays an attitude of willingness and understanding, it manifests itself by the person having an open mind and regarding
your opinions, faults, likes, and dislikes. In other words, on
a verbal level they are very cooperative. When you exude
this quality to someone, his reactions may be just the opposite from the person who feels on the defensive. He will
unbutton his coat or push it back with his hands in his pockets
or maybe even remove it. Without any verbalization on his
part he is demonstrating that he is very much open to you
and your views. If he is sitting, his manner will be relaxed
with legs uncrossed and with no barriers between you.

Because of the nature of belligerence we would expect it
to be the easiest human feeling to discern in other people.
The opposite is true. In our society one is not supposed to
be disagreeable or to show one's dislikes and antagonisms.
Consequently, in conversations that might ordinarily stimulate aggressive behavior, restraint is exerted. But to the close
observer the true nature of these feelings will be quite conspicuous. For instance, a person who sits with his hand over
his mouth while listening to someone else's particularly

strong viewpoint may be really restraining himself by subconscious force from telling him off in no uncertain terms.
The circumstances will vary, but almost always there is use
of the hands to restrain one's feelings of encroaching aggres-
sion. Whether grinding a cigar out as though you'd like it to
be someone's eye, or rapping a pencil in the palm of your
hand as though it were a shillelagh while being taken to task,
we use our hands in a very primitive way to show our true
feelings. Many of these mannerisms go hand in hand. They
are just a few of the many expressions used by people which
indicate how they really feel. But to the actor they can serve
as a periscope into that secret life which he should earnestly
strive to explore. Of course, these observations are not necessarily true in every case and allowances for prevailing circumstances must be made in order to obtain a true picture.

Enough emphasis cannot be placed on the need for the
actor's awareness of human behavior, no matter how small.
This applies to himself as well as to others. Once he is aware
of the actions of his own instrument, even seemingly trivial
ones as I have noted, his perceptivity and insight will grow
into a sense of reality that is most useful on stage. Self-
awareness is one of the highest peaks of achievement for
every actor; it is also true that as one becomes aware of his
own nervous mannerisms and can trace their origins, they
will disappear almost as fast as they are discovered.

In giving the previous examples of behavior and mannerisms, I in no way meant for them to be used by the actor as
character traits in portraying a role. If such an example were
to be found useful in a role, the actor would first have to
create the inner life which produced it. To do so without
creating the inner life would lead to just another conventional
and worthless effect on stage.

When an actor begins to develop his conscious awareness,
hitherto unknown vistas of enlightenment are opened to him.
These must be utilized by his instrument. It is rare for truly
penetrating insight to occur without conscious awareness.
However, extraordinary personal revelations do occur at
times without any preparation or, for that matter, warning.

These vaticinations as they are frequently called, can be particularly frightening but at the same time can be very useful to the sensitive instrument of the actor-artist. Such an experience happened to a close friend of mine and because of the powerful insight it later afforded her in her career it is worth relating here.

This friend was a very talented actress but like so many people never really had an objective picture of her own physical being. Someone once said that a person is seen in three different ways: (1) the way he sees himself, (2) the way other people see him, and (3) the way he really is. In this particular case my friend was granted all three views of herself and they nearly proved to be more than she could bear.

We were having a late dinner in one of the more fashionable restaurants in New York when she excused herself to go to the powder room which was located up one long flight of stairs. She ascended the wide carpeted staircase, not bothering to notice that the whole wall behind from floor to ceiling was mirrored. She remained upstairs only a short time and then proceeded back downstairs. She said later that her thoughts were elsewhere at the time, but as she descended the stairs she looked up to see another set of stairs leading up. Of course it was only the mirrored wall reflecting where she was walking downstairs, but at that moment she honestly thought it was another staircase.

What she saw in the mirror was a girl walking downstairs opposite her and as we are prone to do when observing someone else, she sized her up for comparable physical attributes. She remembers passing the opinion that the girl she saw on the other staircase was not very attractive. Before realizing that she was actually seeing her own reflection, she had time to get an objective picture of her own appearance. All this happened in the time to walk three or four steps on the staircase. When it finally struck her that she was looking at herself, seeing herself as everyone else sees her, she fainted dead away on the stairs. A vaticination like this is a very rare experience, as may well be imagined. All of us have a picture of how we think we look, but usually it is somewhat removed from how we *really* look; how we *really* appear to others.

Explaining later what had happened to her, she told me that she was still in a subdued state of shock from it. She was overcome with a depression that would remain for several months due to her revelation. Fortunately, this talented actress is very levelheaded and she eventually forced herself to face the reality of a very real situation. She immediately set about to improve her appearance accordingly. This she did not by the image she sees every day in the mirror but by the one she was privileged to see only once.